DING

NING

OOK

TOOL GRINDING & SHARPENING HANDBOOK

Glenn D. Davidson

Sterling Publishing Co., Inc.   New York

Library of Congress Cataloging in Publication Data

Davidson, Glenn D.
  Tool grinding & sharpening handbook.

  Includes index.
    1. Sharpening of tools—Amateurs' manuals.   2. Grinding
and polishing—Amateurs' manuals.   I. Title.   II. Title:
Tool grinding and sharpening handbook.
TJ1280.D29   1985   621.9   84-24121
ISBN 0-8069-7904-6 (pbk.)

Copyright © 1985 by Welliver & Sons, Inc.
Published by Sterling Publishing Co., Inc.
Two Park Avenue, New York, N.Y. 10016
Distributed in Australia by Capricorn Book Co. Pty. Ltd.
Unit 5C1 Lincoln St., Lane Cove, N.S.W. 2066
Distributed in the United Kingdom by Blandford Press
Link House, West Street, Poole, Dorset BH15 1LL, England
Distributed in Canada by Oak Tree Press Ltd.
% Canadian Manda Group, P.O. Box 920, Station U
Toronto, Ontario, Canada M8Z 5P9
Manufactured in the United States of America
All rights reserved

Contents

Introduction

Cutting tools produce best results when kept sharp. The quality of your tool sharpening depends on your understanding of what the cutting edge should be like and how to achieve the desired sharpening result. You need to know which type of grinding wheel, tool setup (hand or fixture), and grinding method to use for each tool. Less effort is required to do quality work when using sharp tools. Added benefits will be personal satisfaction and longer tool life.

The art of grinding is to hold the work at the exact angle (desired degree) and then to move the work freely across the wheel, removing a slight amount of material at a time. By maintaining a well-dressed, trued, and shaped wheel, you will make sharpening a simple task.

One of the most exact machining methods in machine shops and tool rooms is grinding. Grinding has not advanced in the home workshop to the degree that skilled woodworking and carpentry have. This book gives information on grinders, accessories, and methods for quality grinding and sharpening at home.

Relief, back clearance, and rake angles are foreign terms to many who use tools, but they are important elements in the workings of a cutting tool. The wood chisel is shaped to cut and yet still control its depth penetration by the angle behind the cutting edge.

Drill bits must have back clearance and front rake, or they will not cut. The twist gives natural front rake, but back clearance must be maintained when it is sharpened. Each tool is shaped to perform a specific task (Illus. 1).

In the following pages you will find detailed discussions on tool geometry, bench grinders, tool-holding fixtures, grinding wheels, and how to combine these elements for sharpening your tools. Excellent results can be achieved by using bench grinders and grinder accessories for sharpening your tools at home.

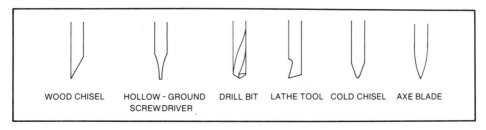

WOOD CHISEL   HOLLOW - GROUND   DRILL BIT   LATHE TOOL   COLD CHISEL   AXE BLADE
SCREW DRIVER

Illus. 1. Six common tools. Each one has been designed to perform a specific task. When sharpening them, maintain their original shapes.

7

TABLE 1
List of Available Grinder Accessories

Accessory	Purpose	Page
Grinding wheels	Grinder cutting tool; a variety is available so you can use the right wheel for the job	26, 33-34
Grinding-wheel dresser	For cleaning, dressing, shaping and removing glaze on grinding wheels	32
Pedestal stand	Take the grinder off the workbench and pedestal-mount it for use elsewhere	38
Wire brush	Use to remove rust, old paint, and polish	38-39
Buffing wheels	Use to buff and polish wood, metal, plastic, or other materials to high lustre	38-39
Buffing compound	Use to aid the buffing wheels for best results, different formulas for different purposes available	39
Flexible-flap wheel	Flexes to sand irregular shapes to save time and make tedious sanding easy	40
Drill-bit sharpener	To sharpen and recondition drill bits (twist high-speed–steel type); rotary action for accuracy	42
Wet sharpener and honer	For sharpening knives, scissors, woodturning tools, axes, and other blades; slow wheel runs in water for best honing action	58, 63
Tool holder	For sharpening chisels, blades, and screwdrivers; holds tools at exact angle; has rack and pinion cross feed	60
Masonry-bit and wood boring-bit sharpener	For sharpening carbide masonry bits and wood spade bits; ensures that both lips are ground the same	69
Router-bit sharpener	For sharpening high-speed–steel router bits; holds router bits in correct relation to wheel and controls index so both lips are sharpened at the same angle	79
Disc-sander	For disc sanding with your grinder; has tilting table and protractor	95-97

TABLE 2
List of Accessories You Can Make

Accessory	Purpose	Page
Grinder mounting board	Hang the grinder on the wall or put it in use quickly	36
Pedestal-mounting fixture	Use for adapting accessories to the pedestal-mounted grinder	37
Accessory bench-mounting system	A setup for changing bench-mounted accessories quickly and easily	101-104
Grinding-wheel storage rack	For safe storage of grinding wheels when they are not in use	105

Each chapter contains basic information, some technical information, and practical methods for sharpening. By learning these methods you will reap the benefits of the tools you paid for. An index at the end of the book is provided for quick reference. Tables 1 and 2 list grinder accessories, their purpose, and the pages where you can find them. By using these recommended accessories and by knowing what to look for when purchasing a bench grinder, you can stay sharp, be sharp, and sharpen.

NOTE: UNLESS INDICATED OTHERWISE, THE DRAWINGS IN THIS BOOK ARE NOT TO SCALE, AND ANGLES HAVE BEEN EXAGGERATED SO THEY CAN BE SEEN MORE EASILY.

1 Personal Safety

Safety considerations are part of our everyday life. For safety when grinding, read and understand the owner's manual furnished with your power tools. These manuals include safety rules to help keep you healthy.

FORESIGHT IS BETTER THAN NO SIGHT

WEAR SAFETY GLASSES

THINK TWICE AND ACT ONCE

WEAR YOUR
SAFETY GLASSES
FORESIGHT IS BETTER
THAN NO SIGHT

When changing cutting tools, always unplug the power tool. In the case of a grinder, unplug the grinder cord while changing the grinding wheels. Grinding wheels are brittle and can be broken by overtightening at installation or by being dropped or abused during use. Do not use a cracked grinding wheel. Some cracks are large enough to be seen with the naked eye; others are not. There is a ring test (explained in chapter 3) to check for cracks that are not easily visible. Blotters used between the grinding wheel and flanges on both sides allow for the uneven wheel surface. They compress at high spots and fill at low spots. The wheel flanges on both sides have a large outside diameter for distributing the clamping force over a large area. Flanges are relieved to make sure the outside diameter contacts the wheel first. You should not use uneven or small washers. If you do not have good ones, order factory replacements.

Illus. 2 shows the sequence of assembly of the flange, blotter, wheel, blotter, flange, and nut on the grinder shaft. In most cases, the blotters are glued on the grinding wheel side and have printed on them information about the wheel.

Grinders come with shatterproof or plastic eye shields, spark arresters, and metal end guards for your protection. Keep them in place. During operation of a grinder, keep the eye shields in place between your eyes and the grinding wheel (Illus. 3). Sparks will sometimes follow the wheel's movement and come out of the wheel guard towards the operator. By adjusting the spark arrester to within $\frac{1}{8}$ in. of the wheel, these sparks will be stopped.

Keep the tool rest within $\frac{1}{16}$ in. of the front of the grinding wheel. As the grinding wheel wears down, the tool rest must be kept adjusted near the wheel face (Illus. 4). The workpiece can be pulled between the wheel and tool rest in a split second if the tool rest is too far from the front of the wheel. Now that you know what the dangers are, you have good reason to remember all the safety precautions.

A face shield (Illus. 5) is the best protection against particles flying into your

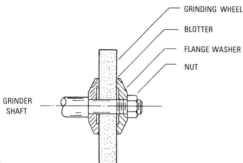

GRINDING WHEEL

BLOTTER

FLANGE WASHER

NUT

GRINDER SHAFT

Illus. 2. Grinding wheel mounted to a grinder shaft with flange washers assembled with relief towards the wheel. The shaft is long enough for full engagement of the nut.

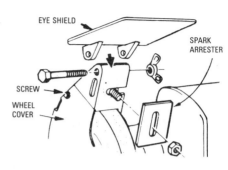

EYE SHIELD

SPARK ARRESTER

SCREW

WHEEL COVER

Illus. 3. Eye shields and spark arresters are adjustable. Keep eye shield between point of grinding and your eyes. Adjust the spark arrester so that it stays near the wheel as the wheel wears down.

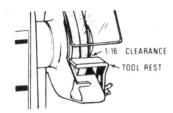

1/16 CLEARANCE

TOOL REST

Illus. 4. A tool rest is furnished as standard equipment with a bench grinder. It adjusts to different angles to suit the grinding you want to do. Always keep it adjusted near the wheel for safety.

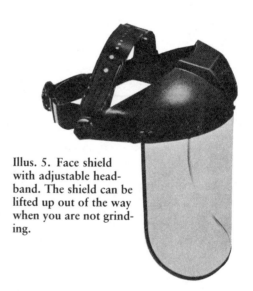

Illus. 5. Face shield with adjustable headband. The shield can be lifted up out of the way when you are not grinding.

eyes and face. The shield pictured is adjustable to fit any size head. Flexible impact goggles (Illus. 6) provide good eye protection. Side shields are a must. The goggles in Illus. 6 fit tight against the face and all around the eyes. This will stop that one in a million particle that comes from left field. Dust masks (Illus. 7) will prevent fine particles from going into your lungs. These face and eye protectors can be uncomfortable for some people, but they are essential for safety. Buy good equipment and test for comfort. After a short time eye protection will be automatic, and you will forget you are wearing anything.

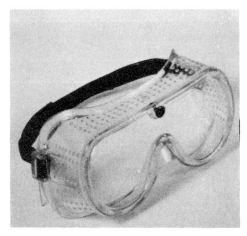

Illus. 6. Impact goggles that fit snugly against the face and have an elastic strap and air vents for comfort.

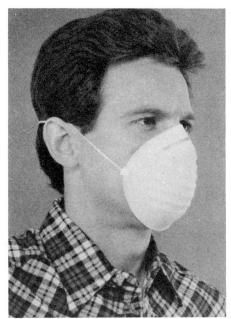

Illus. 7. Dust mask.

When grinding for a prolonged time, especially in an enclosed area, use a dust respirator (Illus. 8). Some models have replaceable filters. We recommend using dust protection any time you grind. Grinding particles are very fine. You can see the larger particles, but the air can carry microscopic particles into the lungs if you don't wear any protection.

Think twice and act once. Grinders and accessories come with detailed instructions. If you do not understand how to perform an operation discussed in this book, do not try to perform that operation. Learn more before attempting to use power tools and their accessories.

Select the proper grinding wheel for the job and mount it properly to the grinder spindle. Then observe the following safety rules.

1. Select correct wheel for your operation. Use "ring" wheel test (chapter 3) and inspect for cracks. Never use a cracked wheel.
2. Never exceed maximum safe speed established for wheel, as printed on blotter. Be sure machine speed is not excessive.
3. Never alter hole in wheel or force wheel on grinder spindle.
4. Use clean, recessed, matching flanges at least one-third of wheel diameter.
5. Use one clean, smooth blotter on each side of wheel between each flange and the grinding wheel. If blotters are not attached to the wheel, you will need to get them.

Illus. 8. Dust respirator with a replaceable filter. This filter will catch dust and other airborne particles that could be irritating to your nose and lungs, but it will not provide protection against toxic substances.

6. Tighten nut just enough to hold wheel firmly.
7. Adjust spark arrester, tool rest, and eye shield, then put on eye protection before starting grinder motor.
8. Read safety rules furnished with grinding wheels and grinder.
9. Every time you start the grinder motor, stand aside for one minute so that your body is not aligned with the wheel.
10. Storage of wheels not in use is important. If you must stack them, separate them with a piece of corrugated cardboard. Another good storage system is wooden pegs on which to hang the wheels. See Illus. 107 for a homemade storage rack.

OPERATING ANY GRINDER CAN RESULT IN FOREIGN OBJECTS FLYING INTO THE EYES, WHICH MAY CAUSE SEVERE EYE DAMAGE. ALWAYS WEAR SAFETY GLASSES OR EYE SHIELDS BEFORE OPERATING ANY POWER TOOL. YOU SHOULD WEAR EITHER A WIDE-VISION SAFETY MASK OVER SPECTACLES OR STANDARD SAFETY GLASSES.

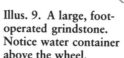

Illus. 9. A large, foot-operated grindstone. Notice water container above the wheel.

2 Bench Grinders

To grind is to polish, wear down, or remove material by friction or abrasion. Grindstones have been around for a long time. My grandfather had a grinding machine that operated by foot pedals. This wheel was probably 3 in. wide and 30 in. in diameter with water in a tin can mounted above to drip onto the wheel. He would sharpen the ax on this machine. Illus. 9 shows one of these old-type grinders.

Illus. 10 shows a bench-type, hand-operated grinder. A geared-speed increase gives more revolutions per minute (r.p.m.) to the wheel than the input at the crank. This type of product is still available today, for those who feel energetic. One hand for cranking leaves one to hold the workpiece. These units have been superseded by electric power grinders.

Using the electric motor as a power source makes bench grinding easy. The grinder uses a double-shafted motor with power cord and switch. Grinding wheels, generally of different grits, are fastened to each shaft so they can be power driven. By adding safety equipment, a light, and a water quench tray, you have a grinder. Illus. 11 shows a bench grinder that has been partially cut away and partially disassembled for identification of parts.

Most bench grinders come equipped with spark arresters, tool rests, eye shields, and on-off switches. Grinders also come equipped with a light and a water quench tray. A large majority of grinders run at 3500 to 3600 revolutions per minute (r.p.m.), although there are a few exceptions, one of which is a variable-speed unit from Sears, Roebuck and Co. This variable-speed grinder can be operated at 0 r.p.m. to 3800 r.p.m. Grinding wheels are marked with a maximum safe-speed rating. Check this rating before installing wheels to be sure your grinder does not exceed this maximum wheel speed.

Illus. 10. Hand-operated grinding wheel that clamps onto a bench. An adjustable tool rest is in front of the wheel.

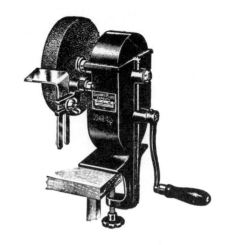

Illus. 11. Cutaway view of a bench grinder. Eye shield and other safety parts, which are attached to both sides of the grinder, are shown on one side only.

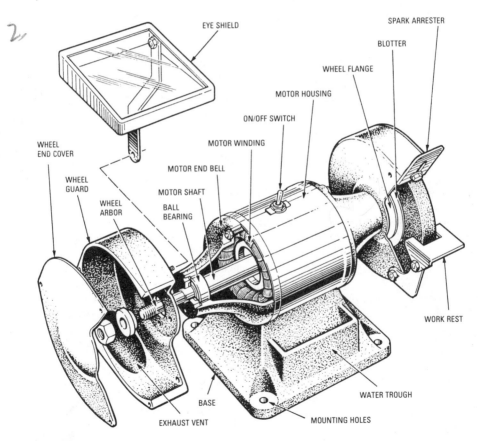

Grinders with wheel diameters of 5 in. to 8 in. and widths of $\frac{1}{2}$ in. to 1 in. are commonly stocked at retail stores. Many stores have more grinders on the shelf than circular saws, routers, or sabre saws. This demonstrates the importance of bench grinders. Almost all, if not all, of these grinders have a fine- and a coarse-textured aluminum oxide grinding wheel attached. Aluminum oxide wheels are of N hardness and are usually some shade of grey. These wheels will destroy a knife, chisel, axe, or any quality cutting tool. Use only hard original wheels for general purpose grinding of soft materials, such as a rotary lawn-mower blade. Using the right wheel for the job is essential to produce the desired results. Proper selection of grinding wheels is covered in chapter 3.

Top quality grinders have permanently lubricated ball bearings. Beware of low-cost grinders that have end play. This side-to-side looseness will make it difficult to do good work. Roller-bearing and bushing-bearing grinders should be checked for side-to-side looseness. Low-cost grinders also lack features such as a light and a water tray. There are grinders on the market with so little power that they will barely pull themselves, leaving almost no power for grinding. On the other end of the spectrum is the Sears 8-in., $1\frac{1}{2}$-horsepower (h.p.) bench grinder. This grinder has capacitor start, lots of starting torque, and a split-phase, induction-run motor with all kinds of power. Most people will not need this much grinder for home sharpening.

By the way, the bench grinder should be one of your first power-tool purchases if you want to use your other power tools efficiently. Don't take the edge off your love of fine woodworking by trying to use dull tools. The cleaning, sharpening, and maintaining of cutting tools can best be done on the bench grinder.

Illus. 12. Two heavy duty ball-bearing grinders made by the Wissota Manufacturing Co. in Minneapolis, Minn. These quality grinders are available from the best hardware outlets and from mill supply companies. They are equipped with 6-in., 7-in., 8-in., and 10-in. diameter wheels. Horsepower ratings are from ¼ to 1½. All have water pots, eye shields, and tool rests. They run at 3450 r.p.m., and most models require 115 volts of electrical power. Some larger units require 220 volts.

Over the past 40 years, important advances in safety features and grinding wheel technology have been made. All grinders must now have large wheel washers, shatter-proof eye shields, and adjustable tool rests to meet published safety codes. Wheel covers must guard three-quarters of the wheel. Grinding wheel manufacturing methods that include quality control and testing have contributed to additional safety. Consumers have also benefited from industrial advancements in grains and bonding materials needed for grinding specific materials.

The list of accessories has multiplied many times in the last several years. With accessories, you can sharpen almost every cutting tool in the workshop. In chapters 3 through 12 many of these accessories are shown.

Before purchasing a grinder, consider the grinding operations you want to perform. Then look at the accessories available that will make grinding a simple task. Sears probably has the most complete line of grinders and grinder accessories. But whatever grinder and accessory you choose, be sure to check the guarantee and availability of parts. Find out if special wheels are available for the grinding of carbide and of high-speed steel. You cannot get the full benefit from your grinder unless you can get replacement wheels of different types for grinding various materials.

The final decision is up to you. Store clerks can only give their opinion, not knowing your requirements. On pages 18 through 21, several grinders are pictured. Some information is given for each in the caption. Only a few of the many grinders which are available are shown. However, these pictures and accompanying information will help you decide which grinder will meet your particular needs. I would not buy a grinder that did not have ball bearings. They are a little less expensive initially but will end up costing more in the long run.

Illus. 13. This Black & Decker bench grinder is equipped with a ¾-in.-wide by 5-in.-diameter coarse-grit grinding wheel, and a 4-in. deluxe fine-wire wheel brush, plus tool rests, wheel guard covers, eye shields, and spark guards for each wheel. It runs at 3600 r.p.m. and weighs 9¾ pounds.

Illus. 14. This bench grinder has ½-in.-wide grinding wheels that are 6 in. in diameter. The motor is a permanent magnet type. It has sleeve bearings and moulded ABS plastic housing. It weighs about 12 pounds. This model has a removable water quench tray.

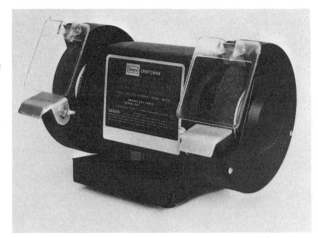

Illus. 15. This bench grinder is rated at ⅓ h.p. but will develop ½ h.p. Grinding wheels are 6 in. in diameter and ¾ in. wide. It has sleeve bearings and moulded ABS plastic housing. It weighs about 19 pounds. This model has a removable water quench tray.

You can do your best work on a grinder that has no end play. To check for end play, hold the wheel with your thumb and forefinger. Try to move the wheel to the right and then left. If it moves, even a little, this is end play, which is detrimental to sharpening. Bronze sleeve-bearing and roller-bearing grinders sometimes have end play, but ball-bearing units generally have none. Grinding requires rigidity; to sharpen tools using accessories, use only those grinders that have no end play.

The gooseneck light on the best grinders is adjustable for shining light at the desired angle onto the work area. Good lighting cannot be overstressed. Some grinder lights come on when the grinder is started. I have had my grinder light rewired so the light can be turned on during setup. This would be an improvement for grinder manufacturers to incorporate into the original equipment. On Sears grinders, the light can be turned on separately.

Illus. 16. This bench grinder is rated at ½ h.p. but will develop ¾ h.p. Grinding wheels measure 6 in. in diameter by ¾ in. wide. It has sleeve bearings, ABS plastic housing, and weighs about 19 pounds. This model has a removable water quench tray.

Illus. 17. This industrial-rated bench grinder is listed at ¾ h.p. but will develop 1.1 h.p. Grinding wheels measure 7 in. in diameter by ¾ in. wide. It has ball bearings, cast-aluminum housing, and weighs 39 pounds. This model has a removable water quench tray.

Illus. 18. This bench grinder is rated at 1.0 h.p. but will develop 1½ h.p. Grinding wheels measure 8 in. in diameter by 1 in. wide. It has ball bearings, cast-aluminum housing, and weighs 49 pounds. This heavy-duty model features a built-in water quench tray, a gooseneck light, and a ⅝-in. diameter motor shaft.

Illus. 19. This variable-speed grinder gives the right speed for the job. You can run slow for polishing or fast for grinding and sanding. Sears variable-speed grinder has a speed range of 0–3800 r.p.m. It has wheels that measure 6 in. in diameter by ½ in. wide, and it weighs 13½ pounds.

MOUNTING THE GRINDER

Use a sturdy bench on which to mount the grinder. Grinding requires a rigid setup. As mentioned before, you will want the grinder near a front corner of the bench for clearance.

Many bench grinders I have seen in use vibrate too much. With the washers and wheels off, there is a perfectly smooth running motor, so the vibration is in the wheels and washers. Take special care when fastening the grinder to the bench. Illus. 20 shows the grinder suspended from the workbench by rubber grommets (bushing). Mounting the grinder in this recommended way will help to minimize this vibration. Tighten the four mounting screws with the same tension so dimension "X" is equal at the four mounting screws.

Next, true the face of the grinding wheels by using a grinding-wheel dressing stick. This will eliminate any out-of-roundness in the outside diameter of the wheels. Use the same dresser to dress both sides of both wheels. Careful dressing will help considerably in controlling vibration.

In chapter 3 other benefits of grinding-wheel dressing are covered.

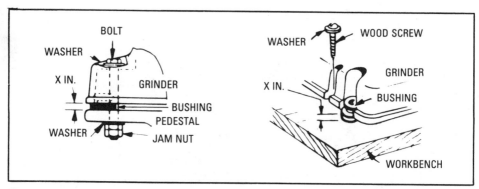

Illus. 20. (*Left*) Mounting the grinder to a pedestal. (*Right*) Mounting the grinder to a workbench. In either case, do not pull dimension "X" down tight but rather follow instructions in the grinder owner's manual. Most will recommend approximately ³⁄₁₆ in. at all four corners.

CONSIDERATIONS WHEN SELECTING A BENCH GRINDER

1. Be sure to use a grinder that has no end play when using accessories to sharpen tools.
2. Wheel diameters of 6 in. or 7 in. give the most desired wheel speed for sharpening.
3. Buy from a company that has developed accessories for sharpening.
4. Be sure replacement wheels are available for grinding carbide and high-speed steel.
5. Check the guarantee; be sure the manufacturer has a good reputation for honoring its guarantee.

WHEN USING THE BENCH GRINDER
OBSERVE THE FOLLOWING RULES

1. Keep adjusting the work rest to within $\frac{1}{16}$ in. of the wheel face, as the wheel wears down.
2. Stand aside and allow the wheel to run idle for a full minute before starting to grind.
3. True the wheel if the face runs out or is irregular.
4. Make grinding contact with a smooth action.
5. Grind only on the face of straight wheels. Use special wheels for side grinding. Light side grinding is permitted on a cup or saucer wheel.
6. Never force grinding so that the motor slows noticeably or work gets hot.
7. Protect wheel when not in use, storing it safely after removal from grinder.
8. Grinding wheels furnished with your grinder are not made for side grinding.
9. Secure the grinder housing to a sturdy workbench using the mounting procedure outlined in the instruction manual.

3

Illus. 21. This high-quality ball-bearing bench grinder is excellent for many uses, including sharpening. Here it is pictured with a drill-bit sharpening accessory.

3 There Is More to a Grinding Wheel Than You May Think

A grinding wheel is actually an aggregate of many small cutting tools assembled into one instrument. These small cutting tools, called abrasive grains, are held together with a bonding agent. Wheels can be manufactured in an almost infinite variety of types by varying the grain type, grain size, bonding agent, and density. Illus. 22 shows chips being cut away by the abrasive grains. The dark connecting links between grains is the bonding agent. Generally, coarse abrasive grits cut away larger chips, producing a rough surface finish on the part being ground. Fine-grit wheels produce a smoother finish.

During the cutting (grinding), the grain particles fracture, presenting new cutting edges. This natural happening reduces heat buildup and tends to self-dress the cutting surface. If the perfect wheel is used at the optimum speed for grinding a particular material, you can keep loading and uneven wheel wear to a minimum.

Grinding-wheel selection is as important to the sharpening operation as saw-blade selection is to the sawing operation, or bit selection is to the routing operation. When grinding carbide, use silicon carbide wheels. When grinding soft materials that are not heat-treated, use a hard wheel.

I have found that only Sears and industrial mill supply houses have the grinding wheels needed to sharpen cutting tools. If other retail outlets have soft aluminum oxide or silicon carbide wheels, I have not found them. See Illus. 23 for a variety of grinding wheels. They are straight-sided and vary in width, bore diameter, and

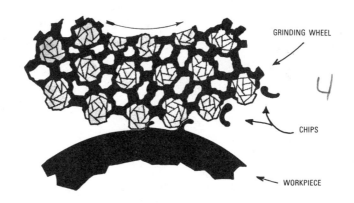

GRINDING WHEEL

CHIPS

WORKPIECE

Illus. 22. The grinding wheel cuts away metal chips from the work-piece. Grinding chips are very fine and will appear as dust on your workbench. In this drawing the chips are enlarged over 100 times.

Illus. 23. These white wheels are ideal for grinding high-speed—steel tools, but because they are soft, they need to be dressed often. These wheels were manufactured by Bay State Division of Dresser Industries, Inc., whose products are available from industrial tool suppliers located in nearly every major city in the United States.

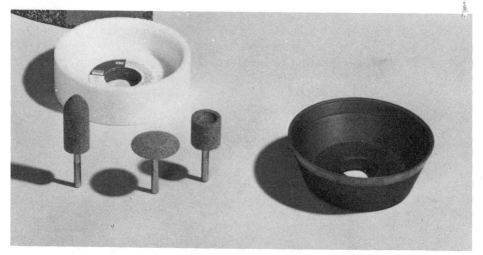

Illus. 24. Three mounted points and two cup wheels. Specially shaped wheels, like these made by Bay State Abrasives, are for special applications only. The dark cup wheel is made of diamond, and the white cup wheel is made of aluminum oxide.

26

outside diameter. There are many other shapes and types of wheels. Some wheels are specifically designed for side grinding. Side-grinding wheels have added strength in the side direction. Cup wheels look like a cup and are for grinding on their sides also. Illus. 24 shows several types of special-purpose grinding wheels, which will not be discussed further.

TYPES OF ABRASIVE GRAIN

Grinding wheels are made of four main types of abrasive grain: aluminum oxide, silicon carbide, CBN (cubic boron nitride), and diamond. It is generally agreed that silicon carbide wheels are harder and stronger than those made with aluminum oxide; however, silicon carbide also dulls more quickly. Wheels made of diamond or CBN are harder than those of silicon carbide or aluminum oxide. In the home workshop you will probably use only wheels of aluminum oxide or silicon carbide. They are both available to you.

Grain size is separated into four main categories: coarse, medium, fine, and very fine. Table 3 shows the breakdown of grain size in each category. A series of separating screens, which allow smaller particles to fall through while catching larger particles, is used to separate grain into size categories. The numbers in the table correspond to the meshes per linear inch in these separating screens. You will probably never need a coarse wheel. The wet sharpening and honing attachment in chapter 6 has a very fine wheel for honing. For most work, a medium or fine wheel is recommended. When you buy a grinder, one wheel will be fine (approximately 120) and the other will be medium (approximately 60).

TABLE 3
Four Main Size Categories of Abrasive Grains

Coarse	Medium	Fine	Very Fine
12	30	70	150
14	36	80	180
16	46	90	220
20	60	100	240
24		120	

TYPES OF BOND

There are five main kinds of bonding agents, namely, ceramic (vitrified), phenolic resin, rubber, shellac, and metal. Most consumer wheels are vitrified, while diamond is bonded with metal or resin. The abrasive can be bonded with its particles close together or with space between each grain particle. Bond material creates a link between each grain. Illus. 25 shows dense and open grain spacing. Both

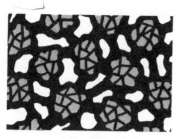 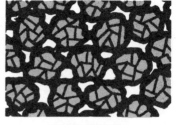

OPEN SPACING   DENSE SPACING

Illus. 25. You can easily see the difference between open and dense wheel structures from these enlarged photographs. Without changing grain size, the structure is changed by varying the volume of abrasive grain.

pictures have the same grain size but differ in volume of bond and closeness of grain. Structure is measured on a scale of 0–14 with 0 being very close and 14 being very open with wide spacing between grains. Open wheels will generally run cooler than closed ones.

WHEEL HARDNESS, OR GRADE

Grade or hardness is the strength of bonding. When the grains are held in place even against a heavy force of grinding, the wheel is very hard. If a light force releases grain from the wheel, that wheel is a soft wheel. The amount and type of bond in the wheel will determine the grade. Wheel hardness is graded alphabetically, in increasing order of hardness; letters A through D represent very soft wheels, and letters V through Z represent very hard ones. Letter K in Illus. 26 represents a soft to medium wheel.

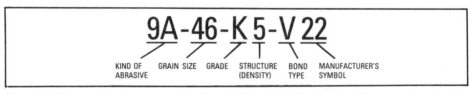

Illus. 26. This number is an example of a grinding wheel description. 9A means that the abrasive is aluminum oxide, 46 means the grain size is medium, K means the wheel is soft, 5 means the wheel is dense, V stands for vitrified bonding, and 22 is the manufacturer's symbol.

Wheels furnished with bench grinders are generally around N on the hardness scale, which is considered hard. This hard wheel is good for snagging heavy nicks, such as those picked up by a rotary lawn-mower blade. Do not try to sharpen carbide tools, knives, scissors, or high-speed tools (router bits, wood turning tools) with this hard wheel. A standard wheel will not cut carbide. If you try, you will only create heat and glaze over the wheel. Hard wheels will burn router bits and other high-speed tools. Overheating the tools will destroy their hardness and render them useless.

Soft wheels give themselves up while grinding. When grinding, only a small amount of material is removed, and the wheel releases grain a little at a time, presenting new cutting edges. This releasing activity helps prevent the tool from overheating and produces a better edge.

TABLE 4

Wheel Hardness (Grade)		Uses for the Designated Hardness	Description of Hardness
A B C D		Not used very often	Very soft
E F G H	I J K L	Use these soft wheels to sharpen high-speed–steel tools, such as router bits, drills and tool bits	Soft to medium
M N O P	Q R S T	Use these wheels for snagging and rough-grinding on soft materials	Medium to hard
U		This hard grade is used in dressing sticks to dress grinding wheels	Hard
V W X	Y Z	Not used very often	Very hard

A grinding wheel is made by combining three major components: bonding agent, abrasive grain, and a filler such as walnut shells. When the wheel is vitrified at an extremely high temperature, the filler burns away, leaving openings uniformly throughout the wheel. The higher the percentage of filler, the more porous the wheel.

29

TESTING AND INSTALLATION

Before mounting a wheel, either new or used, inspect it for cracks. Cracked wheels can fly apart, causing damage and injury. They should be discarded at once and never used. It is a good policy to ring-test any wheel before mounting it on your grinder.

A ring test has been established which depends on the dampening effect of a cracked wheel to alter the sound when the wheel is tapped lightly. Suspend the wheel on your finger from the hole and tap the wheel gently using a nonmetallic instrument, such as a screwdriver handle. Tap the wheel at 45° angles from either side of the vertical, and at 2 in. from the outside diameter (Illus. 27). Rotate the wheel 180° and repeat the test for a total of 4 taps. Undamaged wheels will give off a clear tone. If cracked, there will be a dead sound. DO NOT use cracked wheels. If you are unsure of your test results, ring-test a wheel you know to be good and compare results. Oil-soaked or wet wheels cannot be ring tested because the dampness will deaden the sound.

Follow the grinder manufacturer's safety rules when installing the grinding wheel. By placing blotters between the flanges and the wheel, you will create more driving power from grinder to wheel and also evenly distribute the pressure. Flanges should be at least ⅓ the diameter of the grinding wheel. Assemble the flanges as shown in Illus. 2 on page 12. Tighten the nut as recommended by your grinder manufacturer. Overtightening the nut can cause damage to the flanges and create an unsafe condition.

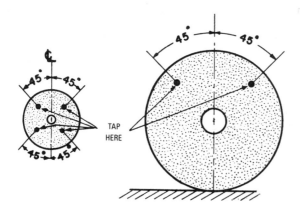

SUSPEND FROM HOLE BY SMALL PIN OR FINGER

Illus. 27. To "ring" test a wheel, tap it at about a 45° angle from each side of the vertical center line and at about 1 or 2 in. from the periphery, as indicated. Then rotate the wheel 180° and repeat the test for a total of 4 taps.

DIRECTION OF WHEEL ROTATION

The sharpest and cleanest cutting edge is obtained by grinding into the cutting edge. See Illus. 28 for the best method to obtain a sharp edge and minimum burr. Bench grinders rotate with the front of the wheel going down, or towards, the operator. However, by placing the grinding contact point of tools with an angle only slightly above center, you can create an unsafe situation. In these cases, you should reverse the cutting edge and grind away from the edge. This will create a small burr, which can easily be removed with a small hand stone. In Illus. 29 the blade should be reversed to prevent a potentially binding situation.

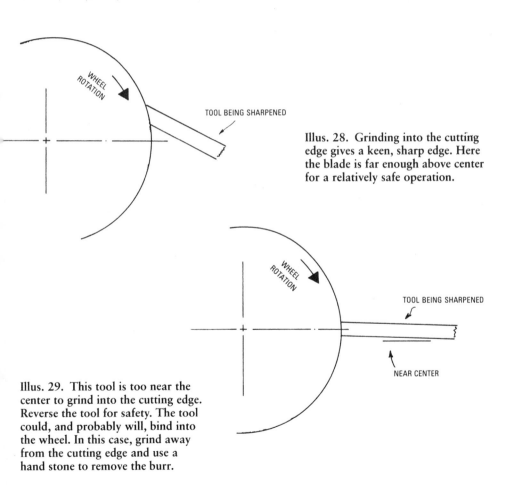

Illus. 28. Grinding into the cutting edge gives a keen, sharp edge. Here the blade is far enough above center for a relatively safe operation.

Illus. 29. This tool is too near the center to grind into the cutting edge. Reverse the tool for safety. The tool could, and probably will, bind into the wheel. In this case, grind away from the cutting edge and use a hand stone to remove the burr.

31

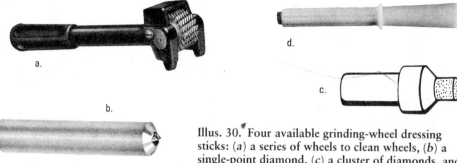

Illus. 30. Four available grinding-wheel dressing sticks: (*a*) a series of wheels to clean wheels, (*b*) a single-point diamond, (*c*) a cluster of diamonds, and (*d*) very easy to use and inexpensive (refer to Illus. 31 for in-use view).

DRESSING THE GRINDING WHEEL

Dressing is a very important part of grinding and sharpening. Grinding wheels load up (fill up with material you are grinding), get dull, and lose their shape. Dressing the grinding wheel is the cure for all three conditions. The dressing instrument must

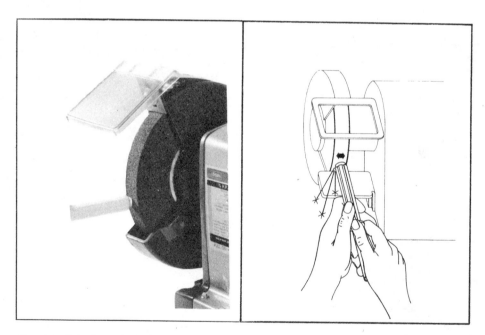

Illus. 31. Grinding-wheel dressing stick. This product has a dressing stone encased in a plastic handle. Use by hand or with the tool holder as described in chapter 8. (*Left*) The contact (freehand) is made below wheel center. (*Right*) A better position with the tool on the tool rest for better support.

be harder than the wheel that is to be dressed (Illus. 30). In Illus. 31 a dressing stick, available at local Sears stores, is shown. This tool has a silicon carbide stone of *U* hardness encased in a plastic handle. Soft grinding wheels are dressed with very little effort. Dressing the popular *N* wheel requires more force and several passes across the wheel face because of its hardness.

Dressing both grinding wheels will also help reduce vibration of the grinder. By dressing the face and both sides of the wheels, you will eliminate the number-one cause for grinder vibrations.

In industrial applications where the grinder has more perfect control of the dressing tool, a diamond dresser would almost always be used. In these applications the grinding machine has a heavy bed and a more positive feed control. An experienced machinist can successfully use a single-point diamond dressing stick freehand. But most of us should use a dressing stick such as the one in Illus. 31. Just about anyone can use this tool and get excellent results.

GRINDING-WHEEL SELECTION

Carbide is a very hard material and lasts up to 15 times longer than high-speed steel. When sharpening carbide cutting tools, you need a very hard wheel made of silicon carbide. Silicon carbide wheels for sharpening carbide are available at some retail outlets. They are usually green in color, although some are black.

High-speed–steel tools are heat-treated to 62–66 Rockwell on the C scale. If, while sharpening, you overheat them to the point where they discolor, hardness can be lost. Twist drills can be sharpened using the coarse wheel of the two original equipment wheels because of the small amount of steel being removed. This points out one of the many variations in grinding and sharpening. You should use soft, aluminum oxide wheels for almost all other high-speed–steel tool sharpening, as shown in Table 5.

This table shows which wheel to use when grinding. Industrial wheels are marked with a code indicating their hardness, grain, bond, structure, and method of manufacturing (Illus. 26). Consumer wheels are not as well marked. Color can help identify the type of wheel. Catalog descriptions and wheel description numbers (Illus. 26) also help.

You can do 95 percent of all the sharpening needed by purchasing two wheels in addition to the ones that came with the grinder. This makes four in your sharpening arsenal:

1. hard, aluminum oxide—fine
2. hard, aluminum oxide—coarse
3. soft, aluminum oxide—pink
4. silicon carbide—green

TABLE 5

A chart to help you select the proper wheel for the job. Grey wheels are included with new grinders.

Type of Tool	Tool Material	Recommended Type of Wheel
Drill bits		
Twist	High-speed steel	Aluminum oxide (grey)
Spade boring	High-speed steel	Aluminum oxide (grey)
Masonry	Cutting edge is carbide	Silicon carbide (green)
Lathe tool bits	High-speed steel	Soft, aluminum oxide (pink or white)
Chisels	High-speed steel	Soft, aluminum oxide (pink or white)
Router bits		
High-speed steel	High-speed steel	Soft, aluminum oxide (pink or white)
Carbide tipped	Cutting edge is carbide	Silicon carbide (green)
Rotary lawn-mower blades	Nonheat-treated steel	Aluminum oxide (grey)
Scissors and snips	Steel is tough (not file hard)	Aluminum oxide (pink or white)

4 Basic Accessories for Bench Grinders

Many general merchandise stores have more grinders on display than circular saws and routers, but they do not have many accessories for the grinders. Sears has the most complete line of grinder accessories that I have seen. Basic accessories and their applications are discussed in this chapter. Later chapters will cover specific sharpening techniques for individual tools.

MOUNTING FIXTURE

Bench space is generally in short supply in the home workshop. I like to clear the deck and work with a clean bench each time I begin a new project. The following simple but useful fixture can be easily made to free the bench of the grinder when not in use: fasten your bench grinder to a 1-in.-thick piece of plywood and suspend the grinder from the plywood with the rubber grommets (bushing), as instructed in the grinder instructions, just as if this board were the bench. C-clamp the plywood to the bench top when using the grinder. When not in use, the grinder and plywood should be put on a shelf, which will free the bench for other uses. In Illus. 32 is a homemade grinder mounting board and an optional 2 × 4 fastened to the bottom. With the use of this mounting board, the grinder can be C-clamped to the bench or stored out of the way in seconds. The grommets are always in place, and the workbench can be used for other projects. Use large hooks for storing the grinder on a wall. Make 1-in. holes in the mounting board.

The optional 2 × 4, if used, should be fastened securely under the mounting board, located directly below the grinder motor. Clamp the 2 × 4 with a large vise, such as a wood vise. Be sure to glue and screw the fixture together for a rigid assembly.

PEDESTAL

Floor pedestal stands are available for bench grinders (Illus. 34). A pedestal will save bench space and leave the grinder available at all times. Cast-iron pedestals are very rigid and do not flex at the floor. This allows them to rock and creates an unstable condition if you do not fasten them to the floor. The pedestal made of steel-tubing construction will flex to the floor and remain portable. This seems to have some merit. To use bench-mounted accessories, such as those discussed in chap-

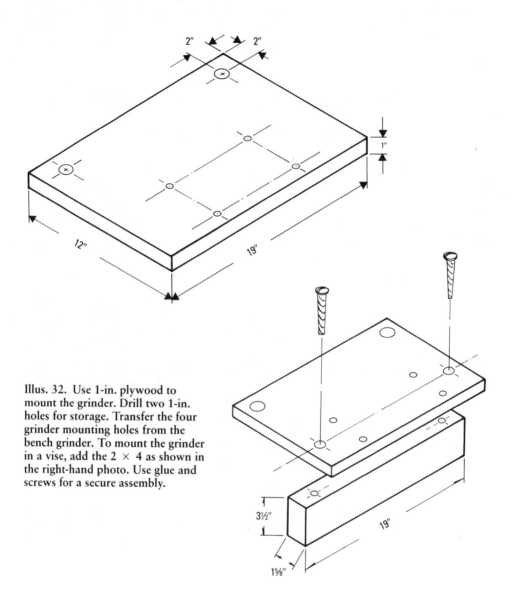

Illus. 32. Use 1-in. plywood to mount the grinder. Drill two 1-in. holes for storage. Transfer the four grinder mounting holes from the bench grinder. To mount the grinder in a vise, add the 2 × 4 as shown in the right-hand photo. Use glue and screws for a secure assembly.

ters 5 through 9, on a pedestal mounted grinder, you can construct a simple wood fixture (Illus. 33). Use 1-in.-thick plywood with 2 × 4 stiffening boards around the perimeter. Transfer clearance-hole locations from the grinder base and drill them $\frac{1}{16}$ in. larger than the mounting bolts. Assemble the fixture between the pedestal and grinder. Don't forget the grommets. Accessories are then mounted to the fixture as if it were the bench.

Pedestals should be used only when there is a specific reason. The best and safest grinding is done on a sturdy bench. By constructing the mounting fixture shown on this page, you will produce a sturdy setup while maintaining a cleared bench area.

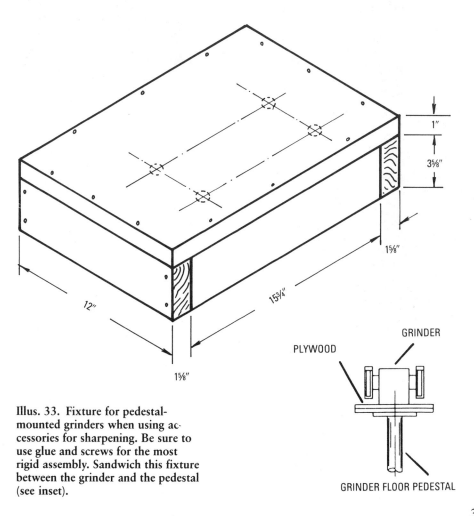

Illus. 33. Fixture for pedestal-mounted grinders when using accessories for sharpening. Be sure to use glue and screws for the most rigid assembly. Sandwich this fixture between the grinder and the pedestal (see inset).

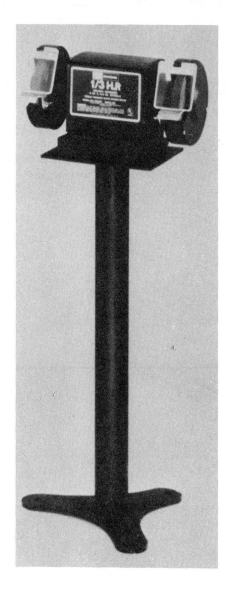

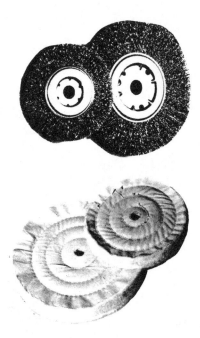

Illus. 34. Pedestals for bench grinders. They free the bench for other uses.

Illus. 35. Wire brushes and buffing wheels. High-quality products may be expensive at first, but they will save you money in the end.

BUFFING AND BRUSHING

Power brushing is used in industrial plants for deburring, scale removal, finishing, and cleaning. These operations are also helpful at home. The grinder motor is an excellent power source.

Wire brushes (Illus. 35) come in several diameters and in fine and coarse textures. Large-diameter brushes with fine wire are best for polishing metal to a high lustre, while small brushes will actually cut material. Thirty-six-hundred revolutions per minute is too fast for brushing. Sears's new variable-speed grinder is excellent for wire brushing. When you have considerable surface area to brush, use two or three stacked in tandem. Quality of wire and method of securing the wire at the wheel hub will make the difference between a high-quality product and a poor one. Sears's wire brushes are made of good-quality heat-treated wire. Each strand of wire goes to the center and is bent back to the outside diameter for secure clamping of each strand.

Buffing and polishing can also be accomplished with the bench grinder as a power source. Cotton wheels are available in several diameters and thicknesses. The resulting surface finish will depend on time, surface speed, compound, and pressure. Bias-type construction has several advantages over square-cut buffs, two of which are a longer life and a cleaner operation as a result of less fraying and ravelling.

Four basic types of buffing compounds for polishing wheels are available for metal, plastic, wood, or rubber. A shiny, lustrous finish can be produced on most materials by using the appropriate formula. Compounds are available in paste and dry-cake consistency. In either case, apply the material to the buffing wheel, and it will transfer to the workpiece. See Table 6 for a list of materials and the compounds that should be used to buff them.

TABLE 6

Material to be Polished	Compound
Copper, brass, aluminum, zinc	Tripoli
Stainless steel	White rouge
Gold, silver, platinum, brass	Red brillo rouge
Cutlery, tin plate, soft-metal alloy	Crocus compound
Steel, plastic, rubber, lacquered surface	Red rouge (general purpose)

Illus. 36. Abrasive flexible-flap wheels, when attached to a bench grinder, make tedious jobs, like sanding, easy. They also help maintain your tools.

FLEXIBLE-FLAP SANDING

Hundreds of tightly packed rectangular pieces of abrasive material assembled together make up a flap wheel. The coated abrasive flap strips can be cut to any length or width. They are then assembled at right angles to the center hole so the abrasive side will contact the workpiece. Flap wheels are long-lasting and will blend surfaces beautifully. The strips will conform to irregular shapes, such as those that are rounded or contoured. Using the bench grinder with a flexible-flap wheel will make a tedious sanding job quick and easy. The accessory (Illus. 36) has been used in industry for years and is now available to the do-it-yourselfer.

5 Sharpening Drill Bits

Most do-it-yourselfers need to sharpen drill bits, but only a few can sharpen a drill by hand. There are many types of drills; the most common are standard twist, carbide masonry, spade and brad point. A variety of accessories is available to sharpen twist drills, while only a very few are available to sharpen the other types.

A drill must have clearance behind the cutting edge to penetrate the part to be drilled. This clearance is called back clearance or lip clearance. For general purposes a 12° lip clearance is recommended. If there is a negative lip clearance, the heel will touch first, and the cutting edge will not touch the part to be drilled, and therefore, it cannot penetrate.

This chapter includes information on drill bits, sharpening techniques, and sharpening accessories. Illustrations will show you how the drill point should look and how to check the point. Improper grinding of the drill point causes 95 percent of drilling problems. Understanding the geometry of a drill is necessary in order to grind the drill correctly so it will cut properly.

TWIST DRILLS

Very little thought is given to the use, care, and conditioning of the common twist drill. Many do-it-yourselfers store drills that will not cut in a box on the bottom shelf: some are broken, some dull, others will not cut for whatever reason. By purchasing a drill-bit sharpener, these drills can be put back in service. Hold it—not just any drill-bit sharpener will do! Some will not give back clearance. Others require four years at a drill-bit–sharpening university. With others you can get the job done, but the results depend on your skill. On the next page is a drill-bit sharpening accessory (Illus. 37) that works very well with a bench grinder. Bench grinders have adequate power, and the wheel is accessible for dressing when needed.

The standard twist drill is available in various sizes. Sizes are listed in fractions, numbers, and letters, as well as in metric measurements. High-speed steel is used in the manufacture of high-quality drills. Sears now has gone one step further with a titanium nitrate drill. The titanium nitrate coating resists abrasion and corrosion. Chip flow is improved and heat buildup reduced, resulting in a longer life of up to seven times.

Cutting front rake is inherent in the twist drill due to the twisted flutes, as Illus. 38 shows. You need not be concerned about maintaining this angle when re-sharpening.

Illus. 37. Rotary-action, low-cost drill-bit sharpener. (*Top left*) The collet is up for loading or inspection while sharpening. (*Top right*) The relative position of wheel to drill in the side direction. (*Above*) The product is ready for action.

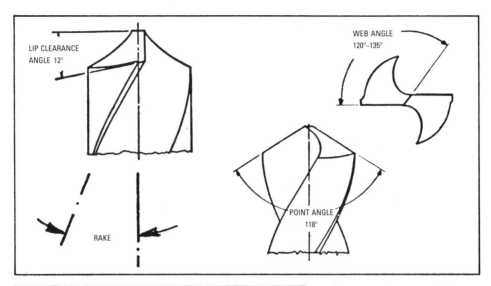

LIP CLEARANCE ANGLE 12°

WEB ANGLE 120°–135°

RAKE

POINT ANGLE 118°

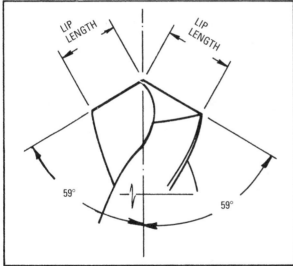

LIP LENGTH

LIP LENGTH

59°

59°

Illus. 38. Three views of a twist-drill point. Lip-clearance angle, for general purposes, should be 12°. Web angle is also important; use 120°–135° for easy drilling. Point angle is not critical. Generally you will sharpen at the angle that was on the drill when purchased (118°). Rake is built into the drill shape and is not a consideration when sharpening.

Illus. 39. When the drill point is on center and both lips are at the same angle, lip length will be equal. With lip clearance and a point on center, your drill will cut on size and will not require much force.

Equal length of cutting lips, lip clearance, and web angle are three elements of a drill bit which must be correct for a drill to cut easily and accurately. Improper sharpening can vary these three to the point where drilling is adversely affected. By using the drill-bit sharpener in Illus. 37, you can control them perfectly. Both cutting lips must be of equal length for the drill to cut on size. When the cutting lips are at the same angle and of equal length, the point will be on center. Because the point guides the drill, it must be on center for the outside diameter to run concentric

Illus. 40. Most hardware stores carry one or both of these drill-bit sharpeners. (*a*) This self-contained model manufactured by Black and Decker does a perfect job. (*b*) This less expensive unit is manufactured by General. It requires a special grinding wheel designed for side grinding.

a.

b.

and drill a clean round hole. Clearance behind the cutting edge is referred to as lip clearance. This angle should be between 5° and 15°, depending on the material to be drilled. For general purposes, a 12° angle is recommended. If the clearance is insufficient, the drill will cut hard, or not at all, and excessive heat will be generated. On the other hand, if the lip clearance is too great, the cutting edges will be weak and break down easily. The web angle should be between 120° and 135°. Proper angle will minimize the power required to feed the drill and allow it to cut freely. Web angle will be correct if your drill has lip clearance and if the lips are of equal length.

Many machinists can sharpen a drill freehand, but if an accurate hole is required, they will use a drill-bit sharpener. The weekend do-it-yourselfer needs a fixture to maintain the three important elements shown in Illus. 38 and 39. Several twist-drill–bit sharpening fixtures are available. Illus. 40 shows some of them. The drill-bit–sharpening fixture shown in Illus. 37 can be used with most bench grinders to sharpen drills of any length that are $\frac{1}{8}$ in. to $\frac{1}{2}$ in. in diameter. Mount the sharpening fixture on the workbench in front of the grinder as pictured.

Highlights of why I particularly like this sharpening fixture are listed below:
1. Grinding is done on the front of the grinding wheel.
2. A fine feed screw gives precise control of infeed.
3. Rotary action gives concentricity to the drill point.
4. Cam action feed gives equal lip clearance to both lips.
5. You can chuck the drill once and sharpen both lips without need to rechuck.
6. The quality of the sharpening job does not depend on the operator holding the drill the same for each flute, or on locating the drill exactly the same twice.

These cover the important considerations in drill-bit sharpening. A gauge is furnished to set the drill in relation to the cam. After gauging, the rest is as simple as turning the handle on a pencil sharpener.

After sharpening, check the drill point. Rotate the drill point up (Illus. 37) so you can easily see the point. If you have the web angle correct, all other elements will be correct also. You will have lip clearance and the lip length will be the same on both sides.

Check the web angle by using a machinist protractor. If you do not have one, compare the resharpened drill with a new one. If you are using some other method to sharpen, after sharpening, check for lip clearance by holding the drill perpendicular to a washer with the drill in the center of the washer (Illus. 41). Be sure the washer hole is a little smaller than the drill diameter. This checking is important because sometimes it looks as if there is clearance when there is none.

The two cutting lips should be equal and at equal angles to the center line. If these conditions do not exist, the drill will cut oversized. One drill lip will also do more work than the other, resulting in a shortened drill life. For general purposes, a 59° point angle (118° included angle) is recommended. For soft material, this angle can be decreased. A steeper angle will require more driving force to turn the drill and a weaker drill point, but this is acceptable, even recommended, for aluminum, wood, and other soft materials. Illus. 39 shows the point angle and length of the cutting lip.

The drill-bit–sharpening fixture in Illus. 37 does not have angle degrees for point angle. You regrind the point by matching point angle to the wheel and resharpening at the original angle. If the drill is broken, use a machinist square to check, as you sharpen, until the point angle desired is achieved.

Very seldom will you need to change the point angle of a drill. Change it only when drilling very hard materials or a lot of plastic, or other soft material. Table 7 shows various point angles, lip-clearance angles, and web angles for the most common materials.

TABLE 7
Recommended Angles for Drill Points

Material To Be Drilled	Included-Point Angle	Lip-Clearance Angle	Web Angle
Aluminum	118–130°	12°	125–135°
Brass and bronze	118–125°	12–15°	125–135°
Cast iron	90–118°	5–7°	115–125°
Copper	100–130°	10–15°	125–135°
Forged steel	118–125°	12–15°	125–135°
General purpose steel	118°	12–15°	125–135°
High-carbon steel	135°	5–7°	115–125°
Plastic	60–118°	12–15°	125–135°
Stainless steel	118–140°	5–7°	115–125°

RELIEVING THE HEEL

One major drill-point problem is heel interference. It seems not much has been written for the consumer on this subject. There can be clearance at the cutting edge when there is still heel interference. This is because of the radius of the sharpening wheel. All drill-bit–sharpening accessories leave this heel problem on all drills over $\frac{3}{16}$ in. in diameter. Strangely, most instructions never mention the problem. A consumer sharpens his drill; it looks perfect, but it does not cut easily. By using a washer (Illus. 41) to test the clearance, this problem can be easily seen. You can grind this heel freehand if you are careful to keep the point and cutting edge from touching the grinding wheel.

The recommended way is to use the drill-bit–sharpening attachment. Two line drawings in Illus. 42 show the sharpening position and the heel-relieving position. In the heel-relieving position, the point is off the wheel, and only the heel will be ground.

You will not have to move the drill-sharpener base to relieve the heel. A swivel feature is built into this unit for this purpose. Loosen the horizontal lock knob and swivel the entire drill and collet assembly until the point is to the left of the grinding

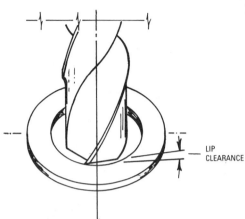

DRILL CENTER MUST BE
PERPENDICULAR TO WASHER

LIP
CLEARANCE

Illus. 41. Washer test to make sure the drill has lip clearance. Drill center must be perpendicular to the washer face.

wheel, probably about $\frac{1}{16}$ in. Reclamp the collet assembly and relieve the heel in the same manner as you sharpened the point. Use a marking pencil to blacken the point after sharpening and before relieving so you can easily see where you are grinding. After you have sharpened a drill correctly and drilled a hole or two, you will be amazed at the results.

Illus. 42. An easy method to grind for heel clearance after sharpening: (*a*) a sharp cutting edge, but a heel interference problem; (*b*) our favorite drill-bit sharpener, in position to sharpen; (*c*) the drill-bit sharpener is swung to the left to relieve the heel, and drill point will be off the grinding wheel; (*d*) dark area has been ground, and now the drill will cut correctly.

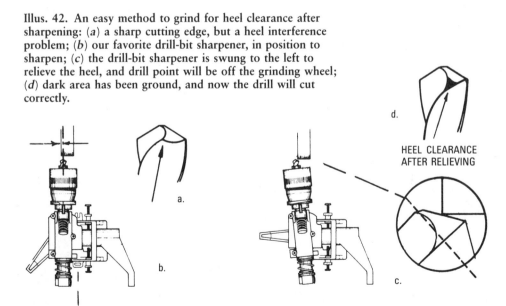

d.

HEEL CLEARANCE
AFTER RELIEVING

a.

b.

c.

THINNING THE WEB

For strength and stiffness, the drill web gets thicker towards the shank. Because of wear and successive sharpening, the shortened drill will eventually have a thick web at the drill point. This is particularly true of larger drills. A drill with increased web thickness can require excessive feed pressure. When this condition exists, it is advisable to thin the web. Thin the web by grinding a short groove on each side of the point. Grinding is done freehand on the corner of the grinding wheel. Illus. 43 shows a drill point before and after web thinning.

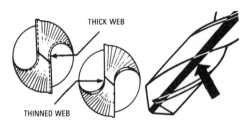 

Illus. 43. A thick and subsequently thinned web. Material has been removed behind the cutting edge on the thinned web. The dark cone represents the web. This shows how the core area would look if the cutting spiral were removed from a drill.

Illus. 44. Relation of drill to wheel when thinning the web. At this angle you can easily see the drill point. The cutting edge must not touch the grinding wheel.

Illus. 44 shows the contact of drill web to grinding wheel when thinning. Do not touch the cutting edge to the wheel. In all cases when you are grinding a tool, darken the area to be grooved by using a black marking pencil. As you grind, the grind lines can easily be seen, and you will have better visibility. If the cutting edge accidentally touches the grinding wheel, you will need to resharpen the entire drill point.

SPECIAL DRILL POINTS

You have probably tried to drill carefully into a piece of brass or wood when the drill pulled itself down into the material. This happens especially when drilling to a controlled depth but not all the way through. This pulling effect can spoil the workpiece before you can react. A small land of $\frac{1}{64}$ in. on the cutting edge will eliminate this problem. The drill must still have lip clearance and a proper web angle; only the front cutting rake is removed (Illus. 45). Use this technique when drilling brass, copper, particle board, or other soft but brittle material. Sharpen the drill as before and grind this small land on the cutting edge by hand. This land

1/64"

Illus. 45. The shaded area is
ground to take away the rake for
brittle materials. It is easy to do,
and it can save the workpiece.

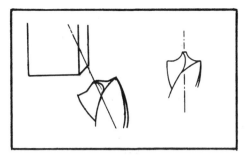

Illus. 46. (*Right*) Special drill point for
sheet metal or wood. (*Left*) Relation of drill
to wheel when grinding. Use sharpener in
Illus. 37.

should be approximately $\frac{1}{16}$ in. long at the outside diameter. Stay away from the drill
point when hand-grinding this land. Dulling of the cutting edge seems strange, but it
works for soft, brittle material. For drilling most other materials, especially steel,
you cannot use this type of drill.

A point for drilling sheet metal is pictured in Illus. 46. This type of point will start
easily in sheet metal and leave less burr at the breakthrough. Use a drill-bit
sharpener (Illus. 37) to grind this special point. Use a dressing stick to dress a
$\frac{1}{16}$-in. × 45° chamfer on the outside corner of the right side of the grinding wheel.
Remount the drill-sharpener base so the drill is at an angle to the wheel. Locate the
drill point on the corner of the chamfer and place the outside diameter of the drill on
the front of the wheel, as shown in Illus. 46. This type of point is self-centering
because of the point's shape, and the outside edge is almost flat.

Since about 95 percent of drilling troubles are caused by improper point sharpening, pay particular attention to this area. A cutting lubrication will help produce
good drilled holes and lengthen the life of the drill. Use a cutting oil for drilling steel
and other metals. Common drilling problems and their cures are summarized in
Table 8.

Center punching is recommended any time a hole is drilled. Even if location is not
critical, center punching makes the drill easy to start and eliminates drill breakage
caused by the walking around of the drill point.

If a regular twist drill is used in wood, the flutes will load up easily. When drilling
deep, you will notice the drill become very hot. Relieve the drill often to allow these
wood chips to come out of the flutes. Relieving means pulling the drill out of the
hole.

The standard aluminum oxide wheels that are used will successfully sharpen
drills on a drill-bit sharpener (Illus. 37). When sharpening by hand, remember that
the drill's cutting lip can become red hot instantly. You may not notice because the

hot area can be only $\frac{1}{64}$ in. wide, but this small area is critical and will ruin the tool. If you keep the tool moving and quench often, it will slow the heating process. This is another reason why a good sharpening fixture is needed.

TABLE 8
First Aid for Drilling Problems

Symptom	Probable Cause	Remedy
Breaking of drill	Spring or backlash in press or work	Test press and work for rigidity and alignment
	Too little lip relief	Regrind properly
	Too low a speed in proportion to the feed	Increase speed or decrease feed
	Dull drill Improper chip clearance	Sharpen drill
Breaking down of outer corners of cutting edge	Material being drilled has hard spots, scale, or sand inclusions Too much speed	Reduce speed
	Improper cutting compound No lubricant at point of drill	Use proper cutting compound
Breaking of drill when drilling brass or wood	Chips clog-up flutes	Increase speed Use drills designed for these materials
Hole too large	Unequal angle or unequal length or both of the cutting edges Loose spindle	Regrind properly Test spindle for rigidity
Only one lip cutting	Unequal length or unequal angle or both of cutting lips	Regrind drill properly
Rough hole	Dull or improperly ground drill; lack of lubricant or wrong lubricant	Regrind properly Lubricate or change lubricant
	Too much feed	Reduce feed

WOOD BORING BITS

Wood boring spade bits and wood pilot screw bits are often made of high-carbon steel. A pilot point guides these bits straight into the workpiece. These drills cut well in wood because of an abundance of lip clearance. Lip clearance should be between 12° and 15°. The Sears masonry-bit and wood boring-bit sharpening attachment mounts on the bench in front of a bench grinder. A fine-feed screw controls the infeed. One-eighth of one turn on this screw will feed the drill in $\frac{5}{1000}$ in. (0.005 in.). Both cutting lips will be ground the same by setting the end stop. When the drill is turned over to sharpen the second lip, place the drill shank against this locating stop. After sharpening both front cutting edges, also sharpen the point by swinging the vee block until the point angle is parallel to the grinding wheel. Wood boring bits are shown below, and the sharpening accessories are shown in Illus. 48 and 49.

After reading this chapter, you may get the impression that sharpening a drill is too difficult to handle on your own—not so. Almost anyone can sharpen drills. Listed below are the things to watch for:

1. Keep the cutting lips from overheating.
2. Use a sharpening fixture designed for the job.
3. Be sure the drill has the following so that it will cut easily:
   a. lip clearance
   b. equal lip length
   c. point on center
   d. correct web angle

When selecting a sharpening fixture, check to be sure you can sharpen a drill with these necessary qualities. Also use equipment that will allow you to dress the sharpening wheel. Rotary sharpening fixtures will give (b) equal lip length and (c) point on center automatically, leaving only two of the four (a and d) to watch for.

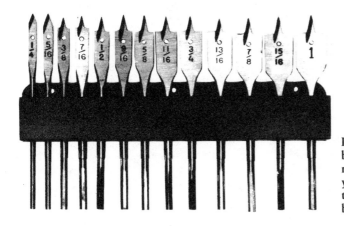

Illus. 47. This set of wood boring bits are sharp and ready to perform. Keep yours sharp, too, by using the accessories with your bench grinder.

Illus. 48. The masonry- and wood boring-bit sharpener can be used with any grinder to sharpen wood boring spade bits. Here, the flat, straight sides are sharpened a little above center to give lip clearance.

Illus. 49. Rotate the tool-holder block to sharpen the point. All sharpening is done on the front of the grinding wheel when using the masonry-bit and wood boring-bit sharpener.

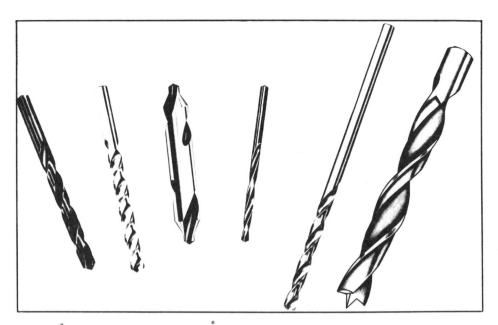

Illus. 50. Drills you can sharpen with accessories pictured in this chapter (*left to right*): standard twist, high helix, center, low helix, extra long, and wood point.

6 Hand-held Cutting Tools

Do better work by keeping hand-held tools sharp. Dull or abused tools are useless and frustrating. Work is a pleasure when tools are organized, clean, and in condition to do their job. You can then concentrate on the task being performed. This chapter will cover a variety of blade shapes, such as straight, convex, concave, and radiused, and methods to sharpen them.

As in the case of grinding all tools, do not overheat them and try not to change the original shape. Their shapes are designed as they are for a reason. Some tools shear, some scrape, some cut, and others work as a guillotine. Remember to grind on the front face, not the side, of the grinding wheel.

Illus. 51 pictures some of the most common tools. Each has its own shape to perform a specific operation. The axe will cut and separate, snips and scissors will shear, while the wood chisel will penetrate as it cuts. Depth of penetration is controlled by the clearance angle of the wood chisel.

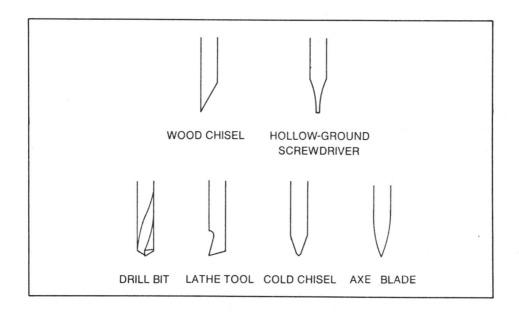

Illus. 51. These cutting tools can be sharpened easily with a wet sharpener and honer. Consider why each tool is shaped as it is, and sharpen it accordingly. Do not change the blade shape in the process.

WOODTURNING TOOLS

The art of woodturning is to create as little dust as possible when removing long, thin shavings with a gouge. The type of wood you use and your expertise will have a lot to do with your success. The parting tools and gouges must be sharp in order to cut while the wood is turned. Touch up by using a hand oil stone to maintain the fine edge (Illus. 52). Professional turners stone the keen edge on new tools before using them and often during use. Scraping will wear out a blade faster than cutting. These tools have heel clearance ground in, but top rake is a function of the angle at which you hold the tool (Illus. 53).

To resharpen the cutting edge, use a wet stone. See Illus. 54 for cutting edges of several tools. An accessory that adapts to the bench grinder with a 220-grit stone turning at 100 r.p.m. (2400 surface feet per minute) and a free-standing wet sharpener are shown in Illus. 55. The grinding wheel runs in water for lubrication. Mount the accessory to the right side of the grinder for honing. You have the left side for rough grinding of nicks.

When sharpening, be sure the wheel rotates into the cutting edge. This will minimize burrs. If a burr develops, it will be away from the cutting edge. Even when touching up the edge with a hand stone, apply the greater pressure when the stone is travelling into the cutting edge.

Illus. 52. (*Right*) This special honing stone has built-in convex and concave surfaces for honing woodturning gouges. The heel of the gouge is lifted off the stone so the cutting edge can be honed to a razor-sharp edge.

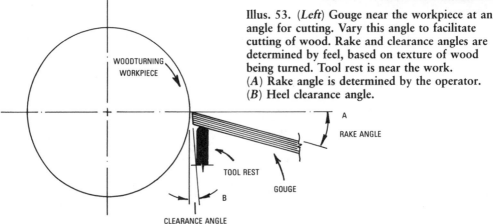

Illus. 53. (*Left*) Gouge near the workpiece at an angle for cutting. Vary this angle to facilitate cutting of wood. Rake and clearance angles are determined by feel, based on texture of wood being turned. Tool rest is near the work.
(*A*) Rake angle is determined by the operator.
(*B*) Heel clearance angle.

WOODTURNING WORKPIECE

A
RAKE ANGLE

TOOL REST

GOUGE

B

CLEARANCE ANGLE

Illus. 54. Four common woodturning tools.

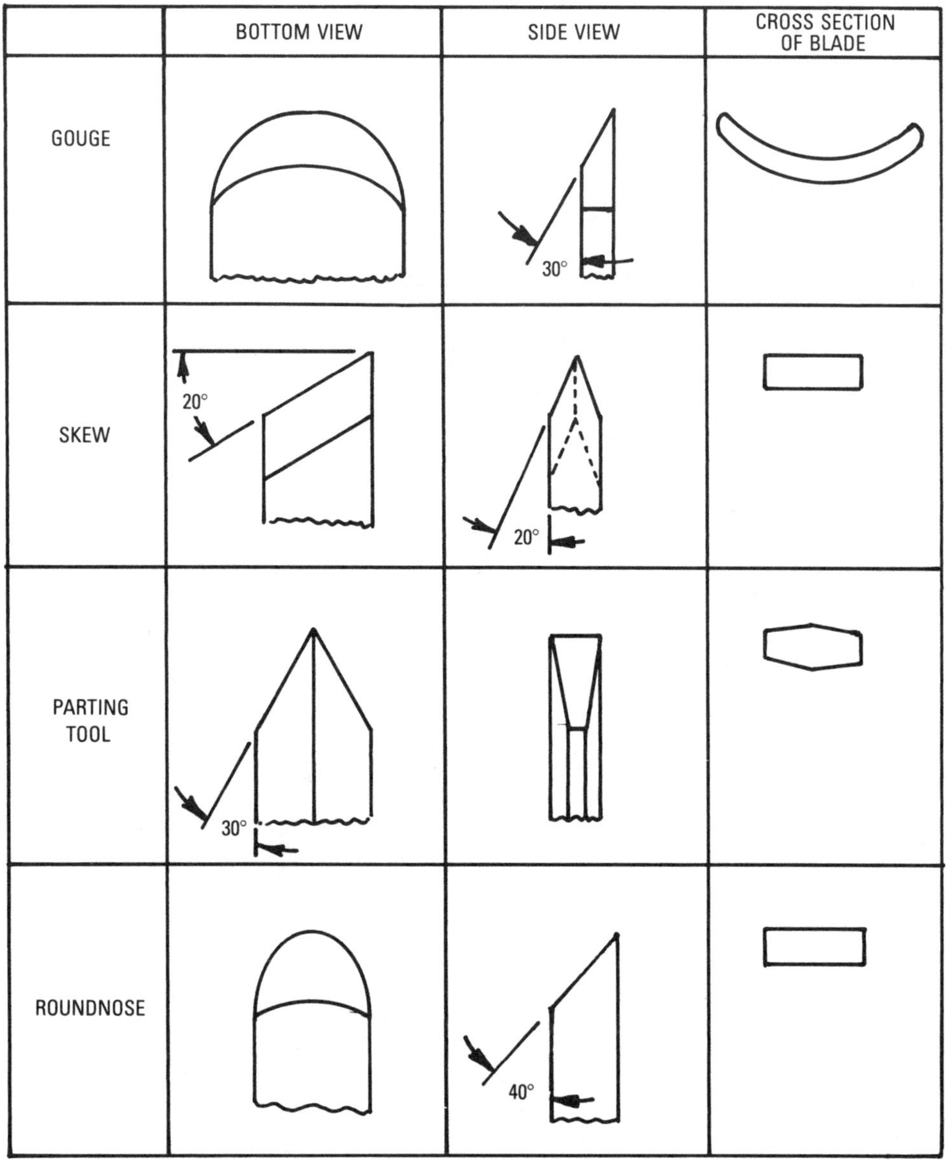

	BOTTOM VIEW	SIDE VIEW	CROSS SECTION OF BLADE
GOUGE		30°	
SKEW	20°	20°	
PARTING TOOL	30°		
ROUNDNOSE		40°	

Illus. 55. Wet sharpeners. (*a*) This wet sharpener and honer, which attaches to most bench grinders, stays sharp longer and makes better cuts between sharpenings. (*b*) The wet stone machine (manufactured by Wen Products, Inc., Chicago, Ill.) grinds, sharpens, and hones tools of all types, including knives, bits, screwdrivers, blades, and scissors. The wet, fine-grit stone wheel prevents burning and burring, and it maintains coolness to produce a clean, sharp cutting edge.

WOOD CHISEL

When a chisel is sharp, the bevel will meet the face at a keen, single line called the cutting edge. We will explain a four-step sharpening procedure: first, square the end; second, hone the face; third, grind the bevel; and fourth, hone the edge of the bevel. Illus. 56 shows a wood chisel and a line drawing that identifies the parts we are talking about.

A wood chisel is sharpened on the end first, so that it can be squared to the sides. Grind as little as possible on the end and keep the end squared to the side. The end must be perpendicular to the sides. Check squareness with a square. Any convex or out-of-squareness is not acceptable.

Second, be sure the face is flat. Check by blackening the face using a marking pencil. Hand-hone the face on a bench stone until the black is removed on the face at the cutting edge. Only the first part of the face at the cutting edge comes into play here. Hand-honing hard material, like a chisel, is time-consuming. Easy does it; continue until the manufacturer's grind lines are removed, and the face is flat.

Third, grind the bevel at about 25° to 30°. You need not change the bevel from its original angle when purchased, although you will probably hollow-grind the bevel if sharpening on a round wheel. Newly purchased wood chisels are sharpened flat on

Illus. 56. (*Right*) The elements of the cutting portion of a wood chisel. Wood chisels are available in many widths and have wood or plastic handles suitable for withstanding the blow of a mallet. (*Left*) A chisel with a 1-in.-wide blade and a plastic handle.

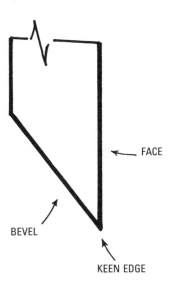

FACE

BEVEL

KEEN EDGE

CARRIAGE ASSEMBLY TO GRIND AT TOP OF WHEEL

CARRIAGE ASSEMBLY TO GRIND LOWER ON WHEEL

Illus. 57. (*Above*) A tool-holder grinding attachment for holding, feeding, and oscillating of cutting tools while sharpening. This model is used with a bench grinder to sharpen screwdrivers, chisels, and other straight blades. It features a rack-and-pinion, side-to-side drive and a fine-feed screw for precise infeed. (*Below*) The two line drawings show grinding a plane blade and dressing the wheel true to the tool-holder carriage. Dressing is discussed in chapter 3; the stick is applied to the wheel slightly below center. The plane blade is being hollow ground at the top of the wheel.

the bevel. They cannot be sharpened correctly freehand. Don't destroy a fine woodworking tool by hand-grinding it on a bench grinder without a guide. Overheating can soften the steel. The edge where the face meets the bevel is a fine line of steel and will heat up in a second on a hard grinding wheel. Use a soft pink or white wheel and an accessory with the bench grinder to sharpen the bevel and to true the end.

A grinder accessory for sharpening wood chisels is shown in Illus. 57. The toolholder grinding attachment was designed to sharpen straight tools, like wood chisels, using a bench grinder. It mounts on the bench in front of the grinding wheel and has a clamping mechanism to hold the tool to be sharpened. The carriage assembly is adjustable to hold the chisel at the exact angle for sharpening.

Before starting the sharpening, dress the grinding wheel true to the tool holder's guide bars. Use a dressing stick (Illus. 31) clamped in the carriage and dress as you sharpen by occulating the carriage back and forth across the grinding wheel. Dressing is done for two reasons: one, to remove any glaze so the wheel will cut clean and cool, and two, so the front of the wheel is straight across, relative to the tool holder.

The fourth step is to put the final touch on the edge so it will be razor sharp. Hone approximately the first $\frac{1}{32}$ in. on the bevel. You need hone only a short distance at the cutting edge. To hand-hone this edge, hold the bevel flat on a bench honing stone and lift the handle slightly (Illus. 58). Work the chisel sideways to hone the edge. To hone this edge using power, use a wet sharpener and honer (Illus. 55). The 220-grit wheel will hone a chisel beautifully. Deburr after honing by using a stropping belt or wood. Do not deburr on the end of a stone because you will lose too much.

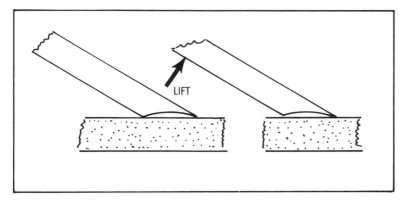

Illus. 58. A fine-grit stone is used to hone the bevel after hollow grinding. In this illustration, the hollow grinding on the bevel is exaggerated. (*Left*) To get the feel for the angle, hold the bevel flat at first. (*Right*) To hone a short area at the cutting edge, lift the handle slightly.

SCISSORS AND SNIPS

Some tools cut with a shearing action without creating chips. Examples of this type of tool are pruning shears, scissors, and tin snips. These tools have almost square cutting edges, but they do have a few degrees of back clearance. High loads encountered when shearing require this type of edge to keep from breaking down.

It is nearly impossible to sharpen these tools on a conventional grinding wheel. If you try to sharpen these tools on a standard wheel, you will only destroy them. It is practical to file and to hand-stone them to remove burrs with a fine stone like the Arkansas. Secure one blade at a time in the bench vise and file across the relief. Cutting should take place with the file cutting into the cutting edge (Illus. 59). The best way to achieve quality of cutting edge and longevity of the sharpened edge is to wet sharpen the shearing tools.

Illus. 59. Hand-hone or hand-file tin snips to keep them in prime condition. Sharpen the bevel by moving it into the cutting edge. Ideally, the bevel angle should be from 20° to 25°. Don't file or hand-hone the face. The line drawing is an enlarged view of the snip blade.

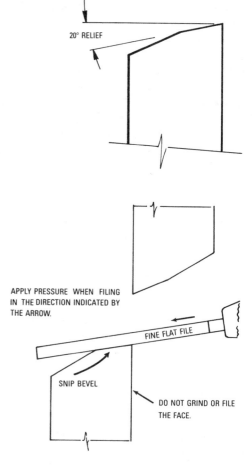

20° RELIEF

APPLY PRESSURE WHEN FILING IN THE DIRECTION INDICATED BY THE ARROW.

FINE FLAT FILE

SNIP BEVEL

DO NOT GRIND OR FILE THE FACE.

Illus. 60. Honing scissors with the wet stone. Use the same approach for all shearing tools. Tip the blade slightly and maintain the tool's original relief angle. On most shearing tools relief angles are between 20° and 25°.

Getting back to the old grind, we will sharpen snips, shears, scissors, and our wits with power. A wet sharpener and honer (Illus. 55) is ideal for reconditioning these tools which shear. Adjust the tool rest for comfort and best visibility. You will get good results because the stone cuts very slowly and will hone the edge. Hold the blade so the grinding wheel turns into the cutting edge. This will prevent the formation of burrs.

Illus. 60 shows a scissor blade and a wet sharpener and honer. The tool rest is adjusted to a comfortable position and good visibility. You can effortlessly pull the scissor or snip blade across the slow-moving wheel. By sharpening often, you will grind very little at a time.

KNIVES AND AXES

Both knife and axe blades need to be keenly honed to give the service we want. On these keen edges, the temper can be drawn out of the steel in an instant, if overheated during sharpening. You cannot allow heat buildup. Also, because of their shape, you will need to swing the blades all the way to their tips to keep them against the sharpening wheel at all times.

A slowly revolving grindstone of fine-grit texture and running in water for lubrication is the perfect tool to use when honing an edge on these blades. A wet sharpener and honer will give these to you. On the Sears model the wheel is open, allowing adequate clearance for axes or knives with long blades.

An axe blade is characterized by two convex surfaces coming together to form a keen edge. This keen edge will cut, and the two convex surfaces will act as a wedge to separate and loosen chips. From the side view, the axe blade is convexly shaped so the cutting edge comes in contact with the wood at its center first. See Illus. 61 for both end and side views of an axe blade.

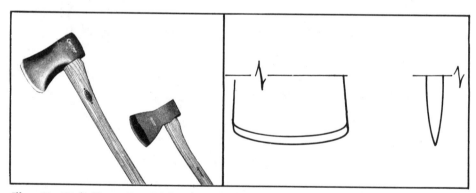

Illus. 61. (*Left*) Two axes. (*Right*) An end and a side view of an ax blade that is designed to cut and split. The short convex sides will split as they penetrate. The side view shows the convex blade with an edge that ensures the center will touch first.

When sharpening the axe, grind on top of the wheel. This gives clearance for the handle as you swing the axe to sharpen its curved surface.

Knife blades are more slender, generally longer, and curved at the point. Hollow grinding of knife blades is desirable (Illus. 62). You can allow the back of the knife to

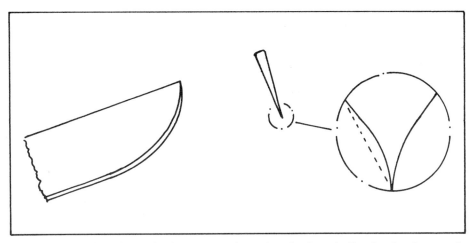

Illus. 62. Knives have long, slender cross sections. A truly sharp knife edge that is properly honed often will outlast one that is neglected until it needs resharpening. The best edge is one that is hollow ground on both sides near the edge. Note that the enlarged knife edge in the circle has ¹⁄₁₆-in.-long, hollow-ground sides meeting at a truly keen edge.

rest on the tool rest as you pull the blade across the wheel face. Use a black marking pencil to discolor the edge to be sharpened. This will help you see the area you have sharpened. I have not seen a better product for honing than the wet stone.

METAL CHISELS

Chisels that are hand held and used to cut metal are called cold chisels. They are designed to cut metals, such as cast iron, soft steel, brass, aluminum, and bronze, which are softer than the chisel itself. Applications include cutting off weld, rivets, and bolt heads. A fine, heat-treated alloy steel is used to manufacture them.

In using this type of chisel, the end is struck with a hammer repeatedly. The end will become swaged over. This mushrooming of the end will leave fragments of steel which can fly off. Regrind a chamfer on the end using a rough grinding wheel as often as necessary (Illus. 63). Do not neglect this maintenance of your chisels.

Standard cold chisels have a double-angled cutting blade and are sharpened on both sides, creating a cutting edge in the center. Use a tool-holder grinding attachment to sharpen them (Illus. 57). Sharpening is similar to sharpening the wood chisel, only you do it twice, once on each side.

Chisel cutting angles are given in Illus. 63. The double angle gives extra beef behind the cutting edge. You will grind only the point-cutting angles for sharpness. Keep the other end chamfered off with a rough wheel as mentioned above.

STANDARD COLD CHISELS

Illus. 63. Maintain a chamfer on the rear end of the chisel that is struck by the hammer so fragments of metal will not fly off. On the other end, the cutting end, grind at approximately a 50° angle.

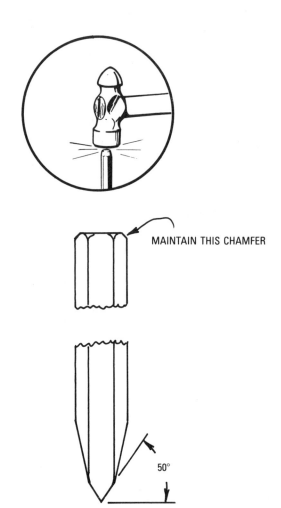

MAINTAIN THIS CHAMFER

50°

7 Masonry Drill Bits

Drills for drilling in brick, stone, concrete, slate, block, and other masonry materials are tipped with carbide. The drill body is made of tempered steel, and the carbide inserts are silver soldered onto the cutting lips. Carbide is necessary because of the abrasive texture of masonry material. There are several grades of carbide, each with its characteristic property. For example, the percussion masonry drill requires a carbide that can take continual hammering without shattering.

Illus. 64 shows several types of carbide-tipped masonry drills: high helix, low

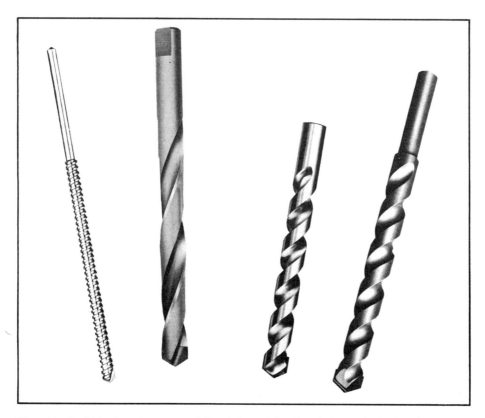

Illus. 64. Carbide-tipped masonry drills (*left to right*): low helix with shallow flutes—for hard work, high helix—designed to pull chips fast, low helix and wide flutes—for chip room, and percussion—for use in hammer drills.

helix, and percussion. These drills will last a long time if used to drill in dry wall. Cement block is also easy to drill into but will wear the drill much faster than dry wall or plaster. Some poured concrete is extremely hard to penetrate. You will need a sharp masonry drill. A percussion driving tool is a time-saver. There are several on the market. Sears has a $\frac{3}{8}$-in., $\frac{3}{8}$-h.p. rotary hammer drill. Drilling in cement is made bearable using this type of hammer drill, a sharp bit, and water. If you need an accurate hole, as for an anchor, drill twice. Drill the first hole $\frac{1}{8}$ in. undersized to break through the rocks and loosen up the material. A second hole can then be drilled much more easily and more accurately.

The regular style is well suited for green concrete, sandstone, or other soft masonry materials. In these cases, the wide flutes provide for the high volume of loose material being created. Faster helix style has more steel support behind the carbide, which supports the carbide insert. Use this style for hard concrete. Both styles are similar in that the tip diameter is larger than the shank diameter. Once the carbide is gone, the drill is useless for drilling.

Enemies of your drill are heat, abrasion, and just plain concrete hardness. Sometimes the sharp edge is gone on the carbide in the first $\frac{1}{4}$ in. of penetration. Using a hammering drill with plenty of water and maintaining constant pressure down with a sharp tool is the best approach. Relieve the drill often to keep chip room and avoid excess heat.

Sears has a masonry-bit sharpening fixture which mounts on the workbench in front of your bench grinder. A silicon carbide grinding wheel is needed to cut the carbide insert. Most silicon carbides are green; but there is also black silicon carbide. By sharpening often, as soon as you notice a decline in results, your drill will last longer. You will also save time and reduce effort.

Illus. 65 shows the drill point on a masonry drill. Just as for the twist drill, rake, back clearance, equal lip length, and proper point geometry are needed. Since the carbide extends out past the steel drill body, you will not be grinding anything except the carbide. By grinding heel clearance on the carbide, the drill will cut. The

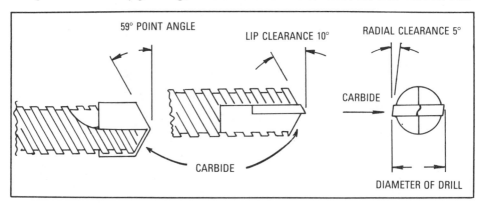

Illus. 65. Masonry drill point.

rest of the drill has clearance by design. Contrary to the twist-drill heel the masonry-drill heel is not ground entirely.

MASONRY-BIT SHARPENING ACCESSORY

To sharpen with a masonry-bit sharpening attachment, place the drill bit in the vee block with the cutting lips straight across (horizontal). Secure the drill body in place. Rotate the vee block assembly to the left until the 59° lip is parallel to the front face of the grinding wheel. The cutting edge must be adjusted above center of the grinding wheel by approximately ¼ in. to give back clearance (Illus. 66). A lip-locating clip is adjusted against the cutting lip, and a drill stop is adjusted up against the end of the drill. These two parts ensure that you will sharpen both lips by the same amount and at the same place on the grinding wheel. The overall view of a masonry-bit sharpener and its relative position to the bench grinder are pictured in Illus. 66 and 67.

Slide the drill bit across the face of the grinding wheel by hand. Use a smooth, steady motion without stopping when the bit comes in contact with the wheel. This accessory controls the point angle and lip clearance. Both carbide inserts will then be ground the same.

Illus. 66. A masonry-bit and wood boring-bit sharpener. The tool-holder assembly is rotated to 59° to sharpen the drill point. A green, silicon carbide wheel is used for carbide.

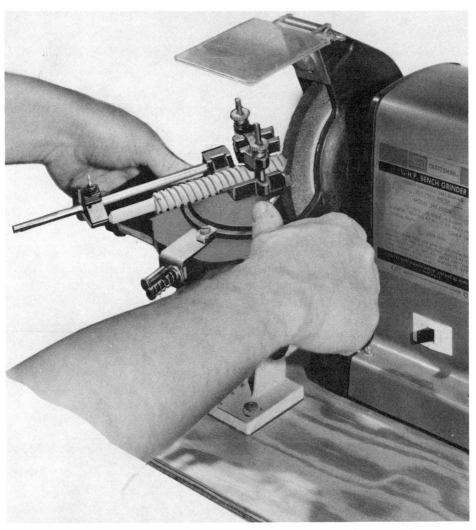

Illus. 67. Drill is sharpened above center of wheel and at the desired point angle. Manually guide the drill point across the wheel. End of drill shank is against a stop so both lips will be ground the same.

After sharpening the first carbide cutting lip, loosen the drill. Rotate the drill 180° and locate the second lip against the lip locater. With the end of the drill shank against the drill stop, secure the drill in the vee block.

Remove only a little material at a time. One-eighth of one turn on the fine-feed screw will feed the drill in towards the wheel $\frac{5}{1000}$ in. The instruction manual gives additional detailed information on using this sharpener.

8 Screwdrivers and Blades

In addition to screwdrivers, this chapter will cover rotary lawn-mower blades and plane blades. All are common to the household and need to be cared for occasionally. You can care for them at home using a bench grinder. Mower blades and plane blades are cutting tools and need clearance and rake to cut easily. Screwdrivers do not cut but must have correct geometry to do their job. See Illus. 68 for several tools discussed in this chapter.

SCREWDRIVERS

Slotted and Phillips screwdrivers are the most common types. Both come in several sizes to fit a recess in the screw head. Use the proper size for the job for maximum driving torque and screwdriver life.

Phillips points come in #1, #2, and #3 sizes, with #3 being the largest. If you use a #1 Phillips screwdriver to torque a #2 screw head receptacle, the tip can be wiped out on the first use. Once the bit is chipped away or twisted, it will need to be

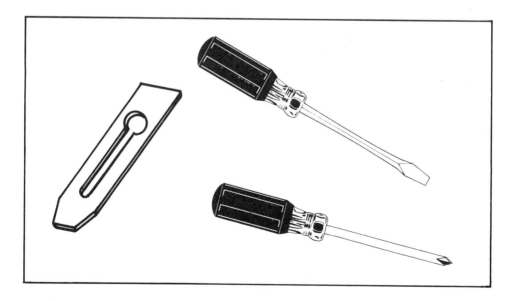

Illus. 68. Screwdrivers and plane blades are common tools in most homes. Their geometry and sharpness are important for proper performance.

Illus. 69. The arrows indicate a side-to-side motion to spruce up the Phillips screwdriver. Use this same square-cornered stone to remove burrs in the flutes. Remove only a minimum of material.

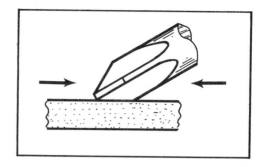

replaced. When the four lands become nicked, burred, or deformed slightly, a hand stone can be used to bring it back into shape. Illus. 69 shows stoning the flutes. To dress up the inside, use a square-cornered stone to clean up the complete flute.

The slotted screwdriver is one of the most misused and abused tools. We use it for prying and chiselling as much as for turning screws. Screwdrivers shaped properly will transmit maximum torque to the screw head without coming out of the slot. The faces of the bit should be parallel to each other for flat contact to the sides of the screw slot. Hollow grinding is recommended for the best reconditioning (Illus. 70).

Screwdriver blades are heat-treated to increase their wear factor and bit strength. Overheating the bit during grinding will destroy these characteristics. If you use an aluminum oxide wheel of *H, I,* or *J* hardness (they will be pink or white in color), it will be easier to grind without overheating the bit. Grind off only a little bit of material at a time and keep the tool moving when in contact with the grinding wheel. These softer wheels are available from Sears or from an industrial tool supplier.

Freehand grinding of a screwdriver is very difficult. I recommend using the Sears

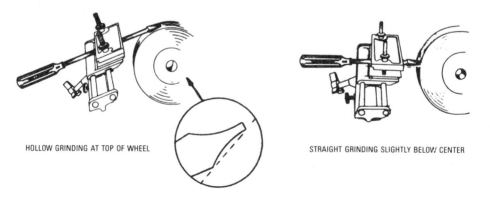

HOLLOW GRINDING AT TOP OF WHEEL

STRAIGHT GRINDING SLIGHTLY BELOW CENTER

Illus. 70. The slotted screwdriver is clamped in the tool holder. Hollow-grind both sides at the top of the wheel. Then reposition the tool holder so the end of the bit is slightly below center of the grinding wheel. This is a fast, fun, and easy way to recondition a screwdriver or a blade, and it produces perfect results.

72

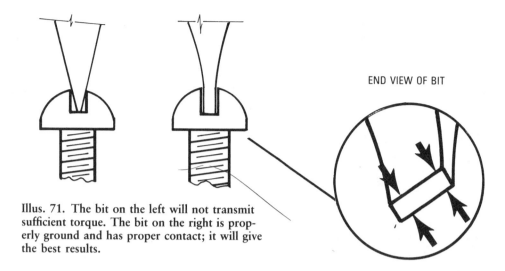

END VIEW OF BIT

Illus. 71. The bit on the left will not transmit sufficient torque. The bit on the right is properly ground and has proper contact; it will give the best results.

tool-holder grinding attachment shown in Illus. 57. This grinder accessory will hold the tool to be sharpened at the exact angle to the grinding wheel, enabling you to hollow-grind both sides of the screwdriver alike. A rack-and-pinion oscillating mechanism gives an even side-to-side motion. Infeed is precisely controlled by means of a fine-pitch feed screw.

After hollow-grinding both sides, true the end in the tool-holder attachment. Hollow grinding was done on top of the wheel with the end past center of the wheel to give a short straight part at the end of the screwdriver. The end is trued slightly below center of the wheel. Stone the tip with a hand stone to remove any burrs that may have been created while grinding. See Illus. 70 for hollow grinding at the top of the wheel and straight grinding the end at center of the wheel. The screwdriver is being held at the exact angle with the tool-holder attachment.

When the sides of the screwdriver blade are parallel and straight, you will be able to transmit maximum torque to the screw. Illus. 71 shows an improperly and a properly sharpened screwdriver blade. The one on the left will easily cam up and out of the screw slot. On the right is a screwdriver blade which will contact the screw slot flat for best results. When viewed from the end, the bit should be parallel, side to side, as shown in the inset in Illus. 71.

PLANE BLADES

If plane blades are hand-honed on a regular basis, they will not have to be sharpened very often. However, if they become out-of-square, nicked, or rounded, you can regrind and hone them. Use a tool-holder grinding attachment (Illus. 57) and also a

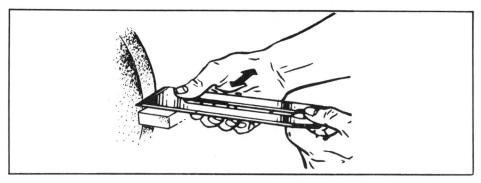

Illus. 72. It is nearly impossible to sharpen a plane blade freehand. I recommend using a pink wheel and the Sears tool-holder attachment.

protractor to check the cutting edge. The end should be squared to the side (Illus. 72), and the bevel should be between 30° and 35°, as shown in Illus. 73.

There are many types of planes, including block plane, jack plane, finishing plane, and rounding plane. A low-angle finishing plane can have the blade at an angle as low as 12°. In contrast, the scraping plane has its blade almost vertical to the workpiece. A very high percentage of plane blades will be ground at about a 35° angle.

After grinding the plane blade using a tool-holder attachment and a soft grinding

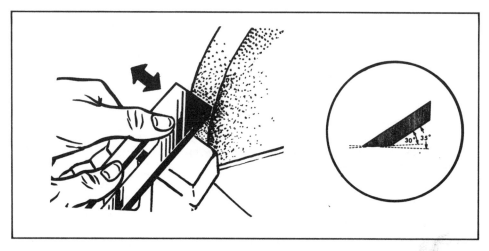

Illus. 73. A plane blade in contact with a grinding wheel. The inset shows a relief angle of 30°–35°.

Illus. 74. The recommended method to sharpen a plane blade on a bench grinder. The tool-holder attachment is ideal for truing the end and hollow-grinding the relief of a plane blade.

wheel (Illus. 74), hone the cutting edge. For honing, use a wet sharpener and honer. It is not necessary to hone the entire bevel. Blacken the bevel and hold it at a slightly steeper angle to the wheel. As the black is worn away, you can see where you have contacted the blade to the wheel. You will have a new short bevel at a slightly greater angle than the ground bevel.

An added benefit of using the tool-holder and wet sharpener is the resulting hollow-ground bevel. Hollow grinding gives a keen edge and back clearance. Honing gives a supersmooth blade which will hold up longer.

ROTARY BLADES

Edge trimmers, tillers, and rotary lawn-mower blades have power-driven rotary blades. These blades come in contact with earth and hard objects, like rocks. Edge trimmers, especially, will contact the sidewalk accidentally. Because of the nature of their use, you can hand-file them into pretty good shape or rough-grind them using the standard bench grinding wheel. Then, stone or hone the final touch. Many people make the mistake of sharpening the edge to a keen edge, thinking they are doing a perfect job. Actually the best edges should have a $\frac{1}{64}$-in. land on the cutting edge. A sharp edge will nick more easily and more severely because it is much weaker. This sharpening tip will give a keen result.

Balance is an important consideration when sharpening these blades since they must turn at high speed. Deep nicks that often require a lot of grinding could cause the blades to spin unevenly. An entire lawn mower will vibrate when the blade is out of balance. Grind equal amounts off both sides when sharpening rotary blades.

To test for balance, use a string and washer as shown in Illus. 75. Hold the string with the washer in the middle of the center hole. Grind as necessary to get the rotary blade into reasonable balance. Sharpen first and then grind for balance on the back of the blade.

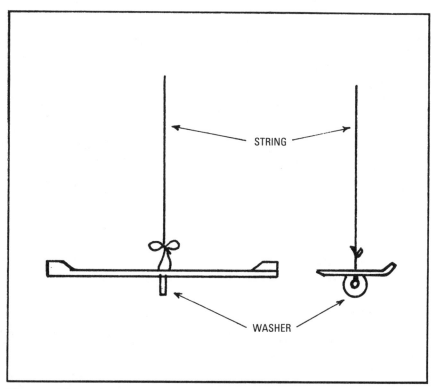

Illus. 75. The washer must be on center and turned perpendicular to the blade to check for balance. Clean and sharpen the blade before attempting to balance it.

9   Router Bits

Router bits are manufactured to precision tolerances from high-speed steel. After grinding, the best quality bits are chrome plated to prevent rust and extend their life. For the avid woodworker, carbide-tipped bits, which have an even longer life, are available. Carbide lasts up to 15 times longer. Some shapes are available in high-speed steel only. When available, carbide bits are the lowest cost in the long run. You should have carbide bits sharpened by a professional.

If you keep your router bits clean of wood tars and hand-hone them after each use, sharpening can be delayed. Illus. 76 shows hand honing on the face of the cutting flute. Use tar-remover solvent to dissolve wood tars.

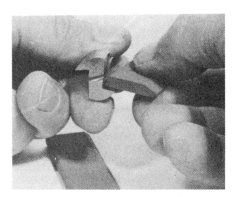 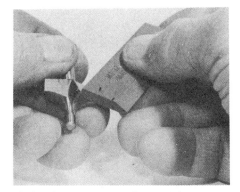

Illus. 76. Regular maintenance of router bits includes eliminating wood tars with tar remover and steel wool. Hone the face of high-speed–steel router bits with a hand stone. This easy operation will delay the need for a complete sharpening operation.

Dull router bits will burn the wood and leave ragged cutting burrs. When you notice smoke or if the router must be pushed harder to cut, the bit is probably dull. You can tell when a bit is dull by looking at the cutting edge. A sharp bit will have a keen edge with the back-clearance angle meeting the front face. When dull, another worn face will reflect light. This worn land will be at the outside diameter of a router bit first and diminish as the cutting edge nears the center. The inexperienced may need a magnifying glass to see this land.

The outside diameter or outside shape will determine the shape of the routed grooves. When sharpening a router bit, grind on the front face so the cut is not affected. This front face is the rake of a router bit, and back clearance is ground into

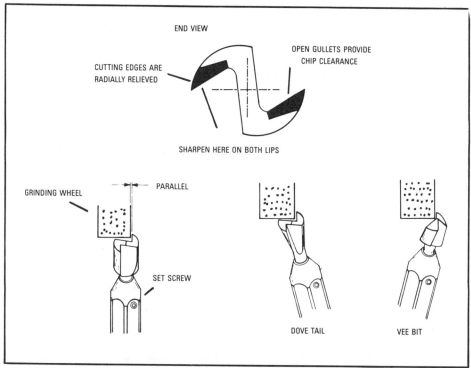

Illus. 77. (*Above*) End view of a router bit shows where to sharpen on the rake angle. (*Below*) The three other drawings show various flute angles. The sharpening fixture in Illus. 79 has adjustments so you can place the router bit in correct relation to the grinding wheel.

the outside diameter. Because the rake angle varies on many of the bits, the sharpening fixture must have corresponding adjustments. See Illus. 77 for three different rake, or flute, angles in relation to the grinding wheel. Note the relationship between the bit shank angle and the cutting rake angle.

Illus. 78 and 79 show two accessories available to sharpen router bits. One is adapted to the router by removing the router base and fastening this fixture to the router. The grinding wheel is then driven by the router at 25,000 r.p.m. The bit is fed in and out to the wheel by hand.

The second is the Sears router-bit sharpener and is used with a bench grinder. It is mounted on the workbench in front of the grinder. Regardless of which accessory you use, a soft wheel must be used to sharpen router bits. Illus. 80 shows this accessory in working relation to the bench grinder. It features a fine-feed screw so you can remove only a few thousandths of an inch of steel per grind. The router bit

Illus. 78. A router accessory to sharpen router bits. It mounts onto the router base, and the stone is driven by the router motor.

is rotated in, across the corner of the grinding wheel. A rotating barrel with two grooves controls the indexing at 180°. This mechanism ensures that both flutes are ground the same. The barrel can be adjusted so the bit is ground at its original angle.

Dull router bits make the router hard to guide straight into the wood. Other problems you will encounter that are caused by dull bits are burning, splintering, heavy burrs, and irregular cutting. There is no need to have these problems because it is so easy to keep your high-speed–steel router bits sharp using the bench grinder. Sharpen both lips the same and use a hand stone to remove any burrs that were created when sharpening. Lightly oil router bits before storing them to prevent the formation of rust.

To remove tar and sap from the router bit, use solvent or alcohol. Severe discoloring caused by burning can be removed with steel wool or a wire brush. Here again, oil lightly before storing.

Bits can be stored in plastic bit cases. An alternative storage method is a 2 × 4 piece of wood with a series of holes to receive the bit shanks. At any rate, keep the cutting edges from banging against each other.

To ensure that your bits give the most, learn to clean, handle, and store them properly. Then sharpen them before they will not cut at all. By sharpening them when they start to become dull, you can get more from the router bits you purchase.

Illus. 79. A router-bit sharpener to be used with a bench grinder. The tool holder pivots to the angle of the router-bit flutes. A fine-feed screw controls the infeed. This attachment makes sharpening router bits effortless. Setup will take a few minutes, but afterwards, the sharpening is very easy.

Illus. 80. Fasten the router-bit sharpener onto the bench so that the pivot shaft is parallel to the front of the wheel. Slots are provided in the sharpener base to make the setup easily. The inset shows dimensions for setup.

10 Circular Saw Blades

Circular saw blades are some of the most productive cutting tools. They consist of a series of chisels arranged in a circle and driven at the center of this circle. As with other cutting tools, a saw blade must have front rake and back clearance at each chisel. Saw blades must have side clearance or set. This side clearance gives the blade room to move through the wood without pinching. Finishing blades which cut with the best finish will have the least amount of set. Illus. 81 shows several

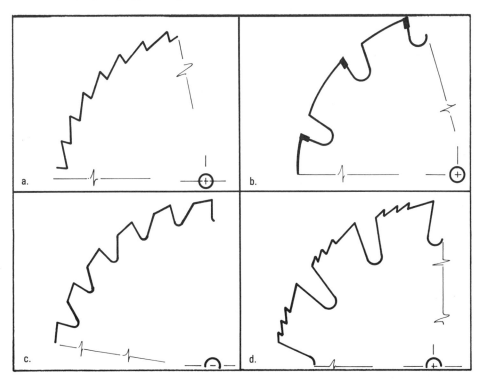

Illus. 81. Four common circular saw blades. Choose the right one for the job. (*a*) Smooth-cutting blade for plywood, soft fibre board, and other sensitive materials. (*b*) Carbide-tipped combination blade for cutting tough materials, except metal or masonry, in all directions. These will outlast high-speed–steel blades by up to 20 times. (*c*) Standard combination blade for cutting soft or hard woods in all directions. The versatile chisel-tooth blade is for making moderately smooth cuts. (*d*) Planer combination blade for crosscut, rip and mitre cutting. It is the best blade for solid woods with a fine finish.

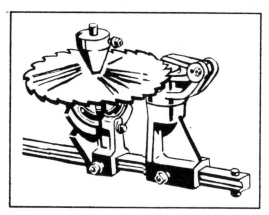

Illus. 82. This fixture is for setting each tooth an equal amount, which is necessary for cutting clearance.

different types of blades. A wide variety of circular saw blades is available from complete-line hardware stores. Sizes range from 4 in. to 14 in. They are made of chrome nickel steel, heat-treated for smooth cutting. You can also purchase carbide-tipped blades for longer life. Carbide is the lowest-cost blade per cut.

Keep your saw blades clean and sharp. Use gum-and-pitch remover to keep them clean, a blade setting tool to give cutting clearance, and a blade reconditioning attachment for sharpening them. A blade stabilizer set to keep the blades more rigid while cutting and sharpening is also available.

Advanced manufacturing methods for brazing carbide tips on saw blades have kept the price for carbide saw blades down. In fact, blade cost is the same or less than five years ago. These tungsten-carbide tips are cobalt bonded and tested for the best performance under the most demanding work conditions. High-quality blades will make more and better cuts than ever before. Thick carbide tips are stronger and can be sharpened more times. Look at the tips before buying and look for thick inserts.

For the best finish, use a plywood or veneer blade. For crosscut and rip, use the blade recommended for the job. In all cases use sharp, clean blades. Illus. 82 and 83 show accessories for sharpening high-speed–steel saw blades. Carbides should be sharpened by professionals. A diamond wheel is used in their manufacture and will work best to sharpen them.

Correct sharpening of the circular saw blade requires five basic steps. They should be done in the following order to ensure that each tooth is doing its share:

1. Set the teeth
2. Joint the outside diameter
3. Grind the hook angle
4. Shape the tooth back angle
5. Bevel-grind the teeth.

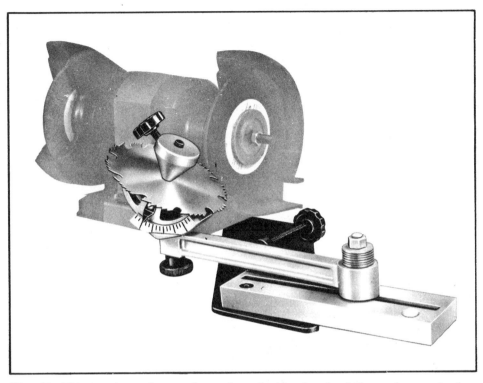

Illus. 83. This saw-sharpening attachment is used with a bench grinder to sharpen circular saw blades. A special wheel comes with this accessory.

With all teeth cutting equally, the blade will last longer, and cutting will be smoother.

1 SETTING THE TEETH

To avoid burning, pinching, or rubbing, make the cutting points wider than the body of the saw blade. Clearance can be achieved three ways. Hollow grinding, as stated, has the saw body ground away for clearance. There is less and less clearance as the blade is sharpened several times. You cannot control or change this type of clearance. The second type is "swaged." In this type, the ends of the teeth are forged to a wider dimension. This expensive blade is manufactured by striking in a press die. You will not set these teeth; proceed to step 2, jointing the outside diameter. The third and most common way to put clearance to the saw blade is to "spring set" the teeth. Bend alternate teeth to the right and left so the cutting tips are wider than the saw body.

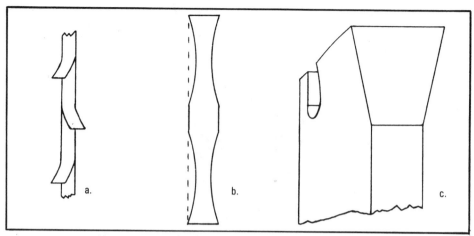

Illus. 84. Three ways to obtain side clearance: (*a*) setting is the most common, (*b*) hollow-grounding, and (*c*) swaging.

When reconditioning a saw blade, use the setting tool shown in Illus. 82. Each tooth will be bent the same amount and at the same angle. Generally, the teeth will be set $\frac{1}{64}$ in. to $\frac{1}{32}$ in. and at a 10° angle. Finishing blades need less set to do their job best, while crosscut blades need more set.

2 JOINTING THE SAW

The first step in saw sharpening is the jointing operation. You must circle-grind the outside diameter around a shaft to get all the teeth tips the same distance from center. Each tooth will share in the sawing operation after jointing. Jointing can be done on a bench grinder using a saw-sharpening attachment, like the one from Sears or from Bel Saw Machinery Co., Kansas City, Mo. You may think your blade is round by sight but do not skip this step. If a few teeth are longer than the others even

Illus. 85. The dashed line is generated from the saw blade's center hole. (*Above left*) Some teeth higher than others. (*Below left*) The heavy lines show a jointed saw blade with teeth of equal height. The inset shows grinding the gullet deeper, which is only done occasionally.

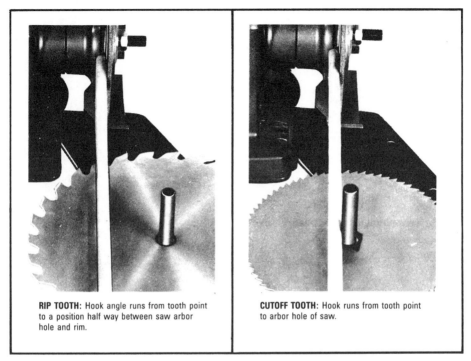

RIP TOOTH: Hook angle runs from tooth point to a position half way between saw arbor hole and rim.

CUTOFF TOOTH: Hook runs from tooth point to arbor hole of saw.

Illus. 86. Hook angles on a rip blade are very different from those on a cutoff blade. Use a straightedge to align the hook angle to the wheel side.

by a small amount, these longer teeth will dull very rapidly because they are doing more work. If a few teeth are dull, sharpening is necessary again.

After jointing several times, the gullet will become too shallow for best chip clearance. Gumming is the act of increasing the depth of the gullets (see Illus. 85). Jointing should be done every time you sharpen, while gumming is only done when needed.

3 GRINDING THE HOOK ANGLE

Illus. 86 shows two different hook angles. This hook could be called rake angle, as we refer to the need for rake on all cutting tools throughout this book. The saw sharpening fixture has a locating dog to position each tooth in the same relation to the grinding wheel. When grinding the hook angle, grind each tooth from the outside diameter to the gullet. Take only a few thousandths of an inch per cut and grind all teeth the same. Finishing blades have a very small hook angle, while rip blades have a large hook angle. Use a straightedge to locate the blade center so you will not change this hook angle.

87

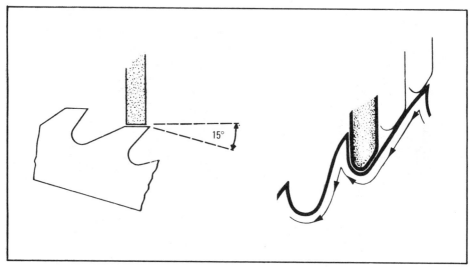

Illus. 87. (*Left*) The tooth back is straight. (*Right*) The blade is turned as it is fed in to grind the tooth back.

4   SHAPING THE TOOTH-BACK ANGLE

Most blades have one of the tooth shapes in Illus. 87. The tooth back is ground up to the cutting point to give a sharp cutting edge. Grinding is done from gullet to point. Take several small cuts, keeping the blade moving at all times. A radius on the grinding wheel is necessary so a sharp corner is not created at the gullet. Saw blades are hardened steel and will surely crack at sharp corners.

5   BEVEL-GRINDING THE TEETH

This final operation will give the front edge its keen edge at the best angle. Adjust the sharpening fixture's arbor 10° to the left and sharpen every other tooth which has the setup. Adjust the arbor 10° to the right and sharpen the other half.

These five steps are fully illustrated and explained in detail in the owner's manual for the saw-sharpening attachments. A special wheel comes with the unit. As with all grinding wheels, dress the wheel using the grinding-wheel dressing stick shown in chapter 3. When sharpening saw blades, keep the blade moving when in contact with the grinding wheel to keep from burning the steel. Sharpen as soon as a land starts to appear. Waiting too long results in grinding too much and shortens the blade life. In addition, regular maintenance will ensure good sawing results. Most of the time, you will need only to set, joint, and grind the teeth tips to keep them in prime condition.

11   Lathe Tool Bits

This chapter will cover metal-cutting lathe tools. Woodturning tools are discussed in chapter 6. To get the best results, as with all cutting tools, the edge must be sharp and have rake and back clearance. Around the house, a square tool bit ground to the desired shape and a cutoff tool bit will be used most often. Tool bits are made either of high-speed steel or are carbide tipped. High-speed tool bits must be sharpened with a soft aluminum oxide wheel. Even then, quench often to keep from overheating the bit. When making a bit from a blank, you must do a considerable amount of grinding. Quenching often is very important so as not to anneal the steel.

The cutoff blade has clearance ground in the blank on both sides. Clearance is necessary on both sides, because of the plunging nature of cutting where material is on both sides of the tool bit. Top rake should be about 10° to 12° for most materials. Exceptions are brass and copper which require 0° to minus 3°. Tools for aluminum can have more than 12° and up to 18°. In Illus. 88 are three views of a cutoff tool. Note, the end can be at an angle for better cutting, and this will also face off the finished piece with minimum cutoff tit.

When grinding a metal turning tool, you must consider the following four angles: top rake, side rake, front clearance, and side clearance. Top rake and side rake are combined to make a resulting compound angle called cutting rake. The two clearance angles allow the cutting point to touch and penetrate the material being cut. Too much clearance can result in weakening the cutting edge to the point where the downward force of cutting can fracture the tool bit. A tool bit from all angles is shown in Illus. 89.

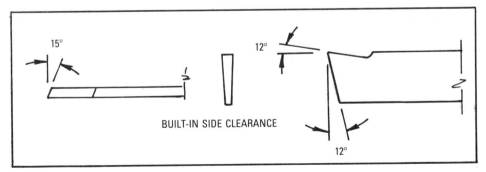

Illus. 88. A cutoff blade with angles for general purpose cutting. This blade has side clearance ground in the blank. Notice the 15° angle on the end for better cutting.

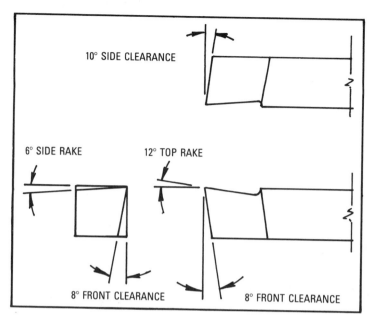

10° SIDE CLEARANCE

6° SIDE RAKE   12° TOP RAKE

8° FRONT CLEARANCE   8° FRONT CLEARANCE

Illus. 89. This lathe tool has angles for general purpose work. They can be adjusted for different materials. See Table 9.

A good general purpose turning tool bit is the roundnose (Illus. 90). For threading, you will want a tool bit ground to a 59° included angle. You will use the same tool no matter what the pitch. Different pitch threads will require only deeper or shallow cutting. When grinding these tool bits for special work, keep in mind that there must be front and side clearance and top rake. On page 94 is a table that lists different materials and their corresponding angles.

A threading gauge is available to easily check the 59° point on the threading tool bit. Illus. 92 shows this gauge in the left-hand drawing. In the right-hand drawing,

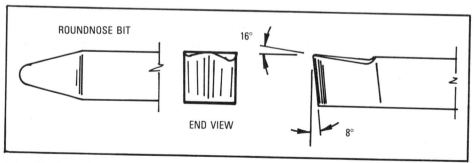

ROUNDNOSE BIT   16°

END VIEW   8°

Illus. 90. Roundnose tool bit with angles for cutting soft steel. Grind the radius to suit your needs.

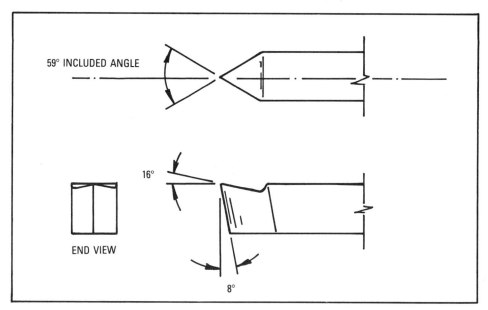

Illus. 91. A threading tool ground at a 59° included angle. Use this shape for all standard threading.

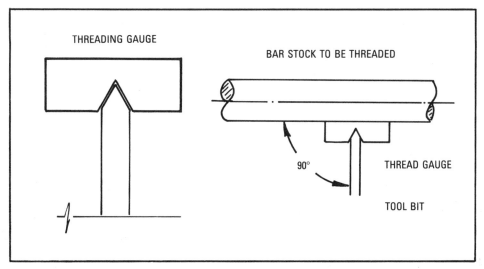

Illus. 92. (*Left*) A threading tool gauge to help you grind the tool properly. (*Right*) Use this same tool to set the bit squarely in the tool-bit holder of the lathe.

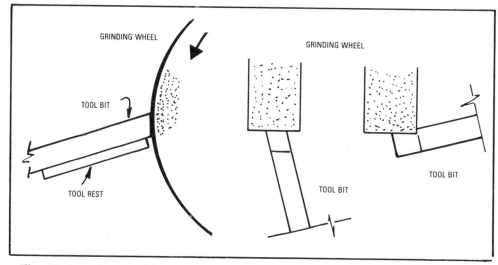

Illus. 93. Grinding a tool bit. (*Left*) Grinding front clearance. (*Center*) Grinding front clearance. (*Right*) Grinding top rake. In all cases, the tool bit is placed on the tool rest.

this same gauge is against the bar stock in the lathe. Use this gauge to get the tool set at 90° to the work. This will give a thread with the thread peak on center.

When grinding a lathe tool on a bench grinder, use a tool rest to support the bit while grinding. In Illus. 93, the tool bit is on the tool rest for support and in relative position to the grinding wheel for sharpening the various angles of the tool bit. Be careful not to overheat the tool. Keep water at the bench grinder for quenching often. It will take a little practice to get the lathe tool bit sharpened at the proper angles. You must first understand what you are trying to achieve. Remember that each angle (rake and clearance) must follow all the way to the cutting edge. If only the first $\frac{1}{64}$ in. at the cutting edge is negative or dulled, the tool will not cut. So, the clearance and cutting rake angles must meet at a fine (sharp) line at the cutting edge. Illus. 94 shows a tool bit, in its tool holder, cutting steel tubing. This particular tool holder is forged at an angle, and the tool bit must be sharpened to allow for this built-in angle. The line drawings in this illustration show a tool bit actually turning a chip.

Illus. 94. A lathe tool bit in action. The chip is cut as the tool feeds across the surface of the workpiece.

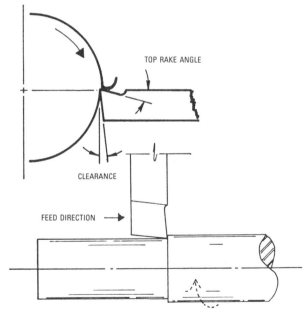

TOP RAKE ANGLE

CLEARANCE

FEED DIRECTION →

TABLE 9
Recommended Angles for Lathe Tool Bits

Material To Be Turned	Front Clearance	Side Clearance	Top Rake	Side Rake
Steel (soft)	8°	8°	16°	20°
Steel (tough)	8°	8°	12°	12°
Cast iron	8°	8°	5°	12°
Stainless steel	8°	10°	16°	10°
Copper	12°	14°	16°	20°
Brass	8°	8°	0°	2°
Bronze	8°	8°	0°	2°
Aluminum	10°	8°	22°	16°
Plastic	12°	8°	0°	0°
Formica or micarta	15°	10°	16°	10°
Hard rubber	20°	15°	−2°	0°

The angles in Table 9 are true angles, measured from horizontal and vertical planes. Some tool holders have built-in angles. You must compensate for the tool holder when grinding the tool bit, if your tool holder has these angles built in. This would mean in most cases adding to the clearance angle and deducting from the rake. Understanding what clearance is for and what rake does will make this compensation easy. Table 9 is to be used as a guideline only. You may need to adjust the angles for particular situations. Use angles that work well. Sometimes you may want to change these angles to compensate for spindle speed and tool-bit rate of feed.

12 More Uses for the Bench Grinder

So far you have read how to sharpen everything—well, at least plane blades, knives, axes, shears, drills, tool bits, scissors, screwdrivers, router bits, wood chisels, metal chisels, and saw blades—using a bench grinder. You've also read how to polish, hone, clean, dress, buff, and remove rust with the same bench grinder.

By removing one of the grinding wheels, you can use the grinder motor for other purposes. In Illus. 95, 96, and 97 are two types of disc sanders. The attachment is designed to fit all grinders with shafts of $\frac{3}{8}$, $\frac{1}{2}$, and $\frac{5}{8}$ in. in diameter. Almost all bench grinders have one of these shaft sizes. Ball-bearing grinders are a very good source of power for this accessory. Very often, it is desirable to sand a piece of wood flat or touch it up at an angle. This accessory has a tilting table which will tilt to 45° and can be secured at any angle between 0° and 45°. The table has a groove for guiding a protractor. This protractor is adjustable to any angle up to 60° either way from 0°.

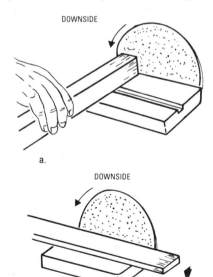

a.

c.

FEED

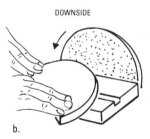

b.

Illus. 95. Applications for the disc sander. The sanding disc will hold the workpiece against the table if you sand on the downside.

95

Illus. 96. The Black & Decker Finishing Machine™ is ideal for removing metal and wood material. It grinds, polishes, cleans, and sands. You can sharpen knives, lawn mower blades, chisels, and hatchets. This versatile machine is equipped with spark arrester, eye shield, 5-in.-diameter by ¾-in.-wide medium grinding wheel, 1-6-in. adhesive-backed sanding disc, and ball bearings. It runs at 3600 r.p.m. and weighs 11 pounds.

The Sears disc-sander attachment comes with a medium-course disc. With this abrasive disc and a bench grinder you can do a lot of work. Always sand on the down side of the disc. Illus. 95a shows cleaning the end of a 2 × 2, sanding a round disc, and through feed; in all cases, the wood is contacting the disc in the location so the table supports the work.

When using this unit with a small grinder, you may need to shim the grinder. A good quality ball-bearing grinder will adapt easily without a shim.

A FLEXIBLE SHAFT

A flexible shaft (Illus. 98) makes the bench grinder much more versatile. These shafts are generally 30–36 in. long and will transmit the grinder power to a chuck or other tool-holding collar. Be sure to operate at the correct speed for the shaft you choose. With a flexible shaft, you can deburr using mounted points, sand, engrave,

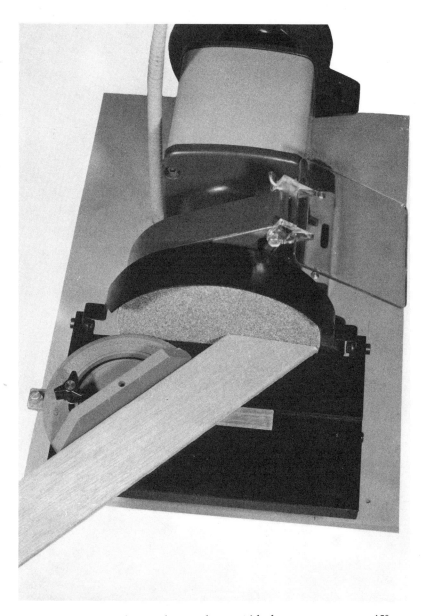

Illus. 97. The Sears disc-sander attachment with the protractor set at 45°
for cleaning the end of a trim board before installation. This protractor is
adjustable up to 60° either way from 0°. For compound cuts, the table can
be adjusted down to 45°.

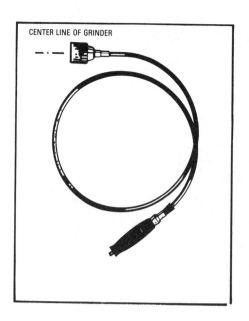

CENTER LINE OF GRINDER

Illus. 98. A flexible shaft to be used with a bench grinder. Be sure to operate at the correct speed for the shaft you choose.

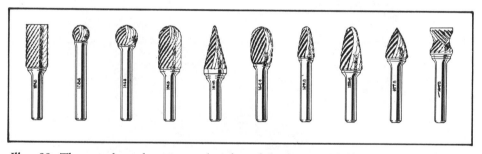

Illus. 99. These ten burr shapes are only a few of the many available. Use to deburr, carve, shape, and sharpen in hard to reach areas.

and polish. Because of the flexibility, you can get into otherwise restricted places to perform these operations. Illus. 99 shows tools you can use. Using a flexible shaft with a variable-speed grinder is ideal. You can vary the speed to suit the job. Sanding is done at high speed, while deburring is done at a slower speed.

USE A MOTOR

Some grinder spindles do not have a motor. Use an electric motor and a V-belt to drive these spindles. You can use the motor for more than one job. Many accessories can be used with these utility spindles.

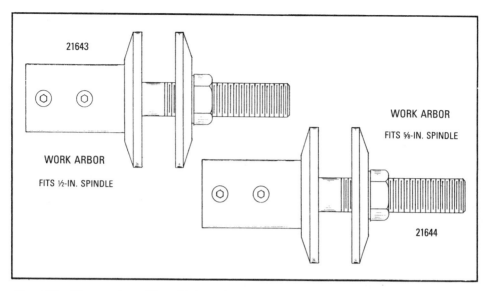

Illus. 100. Motor arbors. These high-quality arbors are machined from solid steel and have powdered-metal flange washers.

This same motor can be used to direct-drive the wet sharpening and honing attachment or the disc-sander attachment. Sears also has high-quality motor arbors for use with $\frac{1}{2}$-in. or $\frac{5}{8}$-in. shafted motors. These arbors are inexpensive and can also be used with a motor for polishing and wire brushing (Illus. 100).

13 A Quick and Handy Setup for All Accessories

Proper placement of the grinder on the bench is important for comfort and convenience. I place my grinder on the front edge and near the right end of the bench, where it gives clearance to the bench when grinding or brushing long workpieces. For small work, I can get close to the wheel for best work position.

Most accessories designed to hold tools and sharpen them are bench mounted. By being bench mounted, they can be used with most grinders. On the next few pages, you will see a handy way to mount your grinder permanently where it needs to be, and where you can still use bench-mounted accessories.

In Illus. 101, the grinder is mounted on a workbench for best everyday, freehand use. It is fastened to the bench properly, using the rubber grommets (bushing). A 30-

Illus. 101. A 2 × 4 is mounted on the front of the workbench, and accessories can be secured or changed easily from this mounting surface. With this setup, you can also use the bench grinder for freehand work. Notice the four holes in the top of the 2 × 4 for securing fixtures.

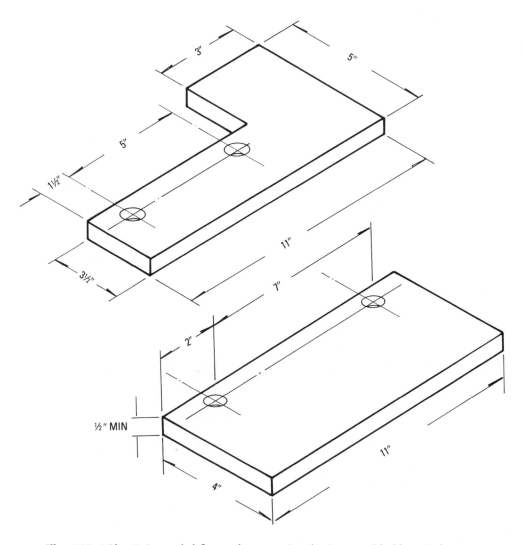

Illus. 102. (*Above*) An angled fixture for mounting the Sears tool-holder grinding accessory and router-bit sharpener. Make two; one for each accessory. Dimensions may vary by ±1⁄16 in.

Illus. 103. (*Below*) A straight fixture for mounting the Sears drill-bit sharpener and masonry-bit and wood boring-bit sharpener. Fasten accessories to the fixture and use the fixtures for storage. Hang the accessories on the workshop wall when not in use.

in. long 2 × 4 is bolted to the front of the bench with four bolts. The top of the 2 × 4 is ¾ in. below the workbench's top surface. Secure your grinder accessories to this 2 × 4.

On the grinder in Illus. 101, mounted as it is, you can use grinder accessories by making two plywood fixtures. Illus. 102 and 103 show these two fixtures with dimensions.

Other accessories not mentioned here can also be used. Once you get started, it's fun to come up with original ideas.

When mounting the fixtures to the plywood, use washers, wing nuts, and $\frac{5}{16}$-in.-thick by 5-in.-long carriage bolts. Carriage bolts will not turn if you drill $\frac{5}{16}$-in.-diameter holes in the fixtures; and wing nuts do not require wrenches. You can change fixtures in a minute. Use the mounting holes to hang the accessories on the wall when they are not in use.

After you have developed a system like this, the accessories are ready to use. When it is easy to get the drill-bit sharpener out and going, we will do it. The couple of hours that it takes to make these fixtures will be well spent. Illus. 104, 105, and 106 show a grinder set up for use with fixtures and some of the grinder accessories.

If tools are handy and well organized, we will use the right tool for the job. Illus. 106 gives an example of a sharpening work center. Take the time to sharpen tools before they will not cut. Regular maintenance is a time-saving way to operate.

Illus. 104. Sears router-bit sharpener mounted on an angled fixture. Mount the accessory onto the fixture after the fixture is in place. Follow instructions for proper mounting.

Illus. 105. Sears masonry-bit and wood boring-bit sharpener mounted on a straight fixture and used here to sharpen a wood boring bit.

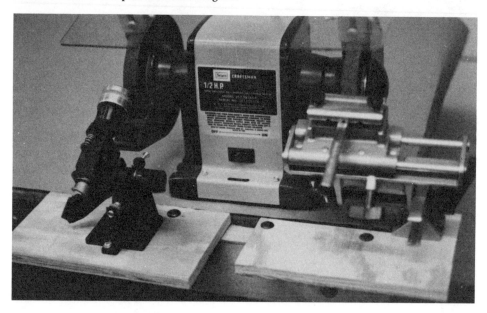

Illus. 106. Sears drill-bit sharpener mounted on a straight fixture using the left wheel. Sears tool holder on an angled fixture using the right wheel.

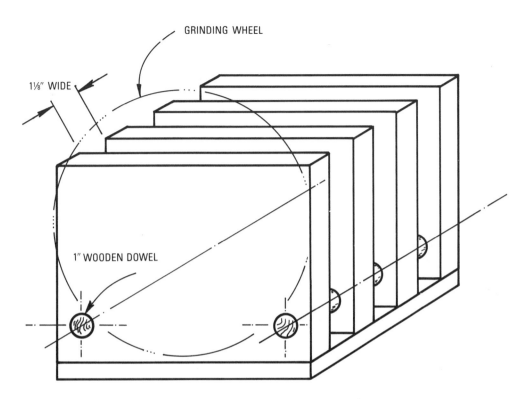

GRINDING WHEEL

1⅛″ WIDE

1″ WOODEN DOWEL

Illus. 107. This three-slot storage fixture is ideal for storing grinding wheels when not in use. The circular interrupted line represents a grinding wheel. The straight interrupted lines represent wooden dowels on which the wheels rest. Note that the dowels are situated high enough so that the wheels do not rest on the base board. Necessary materials include a wooden dowel—1 in. in diameter and 18 in. long, a piece of wood—1 × 8 × 32 in., and some glue.

14   General Information on Sharpening

Your cutting tools will perform best after you have learned to use, handle, store, and maintain them properly. Use the correct relationship between feed rate and spindle speed to produce an even chip. Let the power tool do the work. Do not overfeed to the point where the motor is slowed. Too slow a feed rate lets the cutting edge rub on the workpiece, resulting in fast wear and dulling. Too fast a feed rate will create excess heat and can also break the cutting tool. Learn to spot the dulling of a tool by sight and performance. Proper handling and storage will keep tools from nicking each other and will enable you to see at a glance which ones are ready for use. Maintenance includes oiling lightly after sharpening and before putting tools away. Eliminate burn marks and rust with steel wool. Remove pitch and gum that accumulates on wood-cutting tools with alcohol or pitch remover. Occasionally hand-hone the cutting edge between sharpenings. If hand honing is done often, you may not need to sharpen knives and other fine blades.

SHARPENING

Sharpen by filing, grinding, or honing. I do not recommend that you sharpen by sanding. Sharpen to improve the cutting edge rather than to change the tool shape. The cutting edge is a line where two surfaces meet to form a keen edge. Remove the least amount of material possible to accomplish the sharpening. Most people remove more material than necessary. If a cutting tool becomes battered, reshaping may be needed before it can be sharpened. Generally, sharpening will affect a very small area, and reshaping will not be necessary. Some case-hardened tools have a thin skin of hardened steel. After several sharpenings, this skin is ground away and soft metal is left at the cutting edge. This soft metal will not hold up for cutting. The removal of too much metal when sharpening will shorten the tool's life. Even tools made completely of hardened steel will last longer if sharpened often and if small amounts of material are removed during sharpening. Sharp tools are safe tools.

In the preceding chapters, you have read about grinding wheels, bench grinders, and accessories for sharpening many of the popular cutting instruments around the house. By following a few simple rules and by understanding how a tool works, you can figure out how to sharpen any tool.

Remember:

1. Sharpen slightly, and often, before the tools get dull.
2. Maintain the original shape as designed.
3. Sharpen on the proper surface, so you don't lose clearance or shape.
4. Deburr after sharpening.
5. Store in a safe way.

GRINDING

Grinding is a very productive machining method. The fast rate of metal removal by a grinding wheel will create heat. Heat is an enemy of your cutting tools. Tools made of thick metal can absorb quite a bit of heat before they become damaged. But thin blades, like knives, can overheat in seconds. If a tool becomes so hot that the hardness is drawn from the steel, discoloring it, then the tool is destroyed. You cannot fix a tool that has lost its hardness unless you can reheat-treat the steel. Extreme discoloration is a sign that the tool was overheated. You can remove the discoloration by light grinding, polishing, or scrubbing with a wire brush, but the tool will still be soft.

For example, if you were to overheat a cold chisel and then try to cut a metal bolt, sharpness would be destroyed on the first blow. Grinder accessories explained in the preceding chapters will help you sharpen without overheating. Yes, the tools can still be overheated, but by keeping the wheel dressed, using the fine-feed control screw and proper grinding wheel, you can minimize this problem. When grinding freehand or with accessories, take small cuts and quench in water often to cool the tool. If the tool being sharpened is locked in a collet or other clamping mechanism, dip a sponge into cool water and wipe the cutting edge to control the heat.

Grinding can produce an extreme burr called a wire edge at the cutting edge. This wire edge will be almost nonexistent if the wheel is rotated into the cutting edge (Illus. 108). That is to say that if the back of a knife is on the tool rest and the blade is up with the front of the wheel rotating downwards, a minimal burr will be formed. In some cases, you will not be able to grind in this manner; you will be grinding away from the edge. By grinding a small amount on one side and then on the other you will create less burr than grinding too much at once. Use a hand stone to deburr after sharpening.

FILING

Rotary lawn-mower blades, shovels, hoes, and snips are some examples of tools that can be hand-filed. Files are above 62 Rockwell on the C scale in hardness; these blades are softer than files. Router bits, lathe tool bits, and all carbide bits are too hard to be cut by a file. At their grade of hardness, a hand file will ride

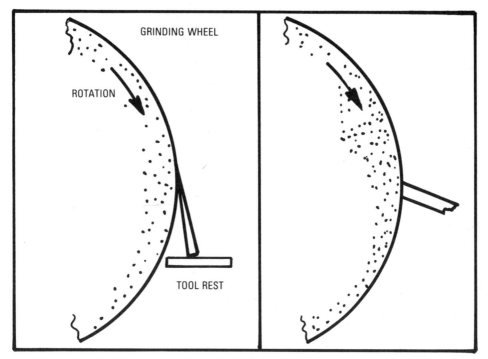

Illus. 108. The recommended tool location relative to the grinding wheel rotation for minimum burr. (*Left*) The wheel is rotating into the cutting edge. A minimum wire edge will be formed. (*Right*) A chisel. A blade that has been sharpened on two sides.

across without cutting, no matter how hard you hold the file against the tool. A distinctive sound, recognizable to experienced filers, is emitted.

You can sharpen a pretty good edge on the softer tools with a hand file. There are over 100 different files and three basic cut types: single, double, and rasp (Illus. 109). Rasp cut is for wood and double cut is for soft steel; neither is for sharpening.

When filing to sharpen a blade, use a smooth, single-cut file about 12 in. long with a flat cutting surface. Clamp the blade in a bench vise and file into the cutting edge. File the back clearance angle only; do not touch the front face. This is important in order to get the best shearing action.

HONING

To hone is to apply the finishing touches—polishing and smoothing—to a sharpened tool. Slight burrs are removed, and a keener, longer-lasting edge is produced.

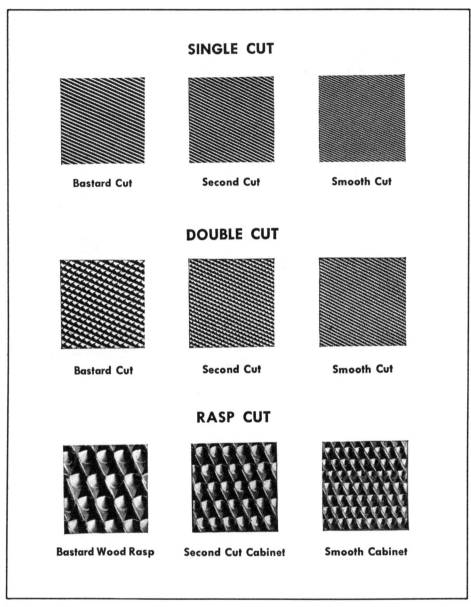

SINGLE CUT

Bastard Cut   Second Cut   Smooth Cut

DOUBLE CUT

Bastard Cut   Second Cut   Smooth Cut

RASP CUT

Bastard Wood Rasp   Second Cut Cabinet   Smooth Cabinet

Illus. 109. Nine types of files. Use the smooth, single-cut file for sharpening. Double cut and rasp cut are for other purposes.

An abrasive stone, aluminum oxide, or silicon carbide is applied at low speed to a cutting edge to perform this operation. New tools are not ready for service until they have been honed. An advanced do-it-yourselfer will hone a new chisel before using it. After sharpening a tool, hand-hone the cutting edge. The life of a cutting edge can be prolonged and the tool's efficiency improved by touching up the edge between sharpenings with a honing stone.

Lathe tool bits and router bits can be hand-honed without taking them out of their clamped cutting positions in the tool post and router collet respectively.

A small amount of oil or water on the honing stone is helpful. Honing stones are very fine, generally 300 to 3000 grit. They can load up with metal particles if used without lubrication, which will suspend the tiny metal particles. After each use, clean off the stone with a solvent and clean rag. Dried oil and grit left on the stone is undesirable. The honing stone must be held flat against the surface being honed to keep from rounding the cutting edge. Illus. 58 on page 61 shows the relationship between a honing stone and the chisel. With the heel lifted slightly, you can hone the bevel at the cutting edge to a fine finish. Hold the chisel firmly and apply pressure downwards as you oscillate the chisel in a circular motion. Hand-honing takes some patience. Don't try to finish in two seconds. You can achieve a micro-fine edge where the bevel meets the blade's face. Hone with a soft Arkansas stone to a sharp edge and then finish to a polished sheen using a harder Arkansas. This is the ultimate sharpened edge.

Several powered honing products are available. They are powered by a motor or grinder or have their own self-contained motor. The wheels turn at 200 to 300 surface feet per minute for honing. Compared to grinding, this speed is very slow. For heat dissipation and lubrication, the honing wheel runs in water. In chapter 6, a honing attachment that uses a bench grinder as its power source is pictured (see Illus. 55 and 60). Using this product, you will very seldom need to touch your cutting tools to a 3600 r.p.m. grinding wheel. I will never again touch a quality knife to a knife sharpener on an electric can opener. Knives should be honed.

Appendixes

Appendix A

METRIC CONVERSION TABLES

Metric to Imperial

Metric		Imperial
Length		
centimetres	× 0.3937	= inches
centimetres	× 0.0328	= feet
centimetres	× 0.0109	= yards
metres	× 1.0936	= yards
kilometres	× 0.6215	= miles
Area		
square centimetres	× 0.1550	= square inches
square millimetres	× 0.00153	= square inches
square centimetres	× 0.001076	= square feet
square metres	× 1.1960	= square yards
square metres	× 2.471×10^{-4}	= acres
square kilometres	× 0.3861	= square miles
Volume (U.S.)		
litres	× 2.1133	= pints
litres	× 1.0567	= quarts
cubic centimetres	× 2.642×10^{-4}	= gallons
litres	× 0.2642	= gallons
cubic centimetres	× 0.0610	= cubic inches
Weight		
newtons	× 0.2248	= pounds
kilogram force	× 2.2046	= pounds
kilogram force	× 0.00110	= tons (short)
tons (metric)	× 1.1023	= tons (short)
Power		
kilowatts	× 1.3410	= horsepower
Energy		
joules	× 9.478×10^{-4}	= British thermal units
kilowatt hours	× 3413.1	= British thermal units
Angle Measures		
radians	× 57.30	= degrees
grads	× 0.900	= degrees
Temperature		
Celsius (°C)	× 9 ÷ 5 + 32	= Fahrenheit (°F)

Imperial to Metric

Imperial		Metric
Length		
inches	× 2.540	= centimetres
feet	× 30.48	= centimetres
yards	× 91.44	= centimetres
yards	× 0.9144	= metres
miles	× 1.609	= kilometres
Area		
square inches	× 6.452	= square centimetres
square inches	× 645.2	= square millimetres
square feet	× 929.0	= square centimetres
square yards	× 0.8361	= square metres
acres	× 4047	= square metres
square miles	× 2.590	= square kilometres
Volume (U.S.)		
pints	× 0.4732	= litres
quarts	× 0.9464	= litres
gallons	× 3785	= cubic centimetres
gallons	× 3.785	= litres
cubic inches	× 16.39	= cubic centimetres
Weight		
pounds	× 4.448	= newtons
pounds	× 0.4536	= kilogram force
tons (short)	× 907.2	= kilogram force
tons (short)	× 0.9072	= tons (metric)
Power		
horsepower	× 0.7457	= kilowatts
Energy		
British thermal units	× 1055	= joules
British thermal units	× 2.930×10^{-4}	= kilowatt hours
Angle measures		
degrees	× 0.01745	= radians
degrees	× 1.111	= grads
Temperature		
Fahrenheit (°F)	$- 32 \times 5 \div 9 =$	= Celsius(°C)

Appendix B

MILLIMETRE EQUIVALENTS OF INCHES

Inches Expressed in Millimetres

Inches	0	1	2	3	4	5	6
1/2	12.7	38.1	63.5	88.9	114.3	139.7	165.1
33/64	13.10	38.49	63.90	89.3	114.69	140.09	165.49
17/32	13.49	38.89	64.29	89.69	115.09	140.49	165.89
35/64	13.89	39.29	64.69	90.09	115.49	140.89	166.29
9/16	14.29	39.69	65.09	90.49	115.89	141.29	166.68
37/64	14.68	40.08	65.48	90.88	116.28	141.68	167.08
19/32	15.08	40.48	65.88	91.28	116.68	142.08	167.48
39/64	15.48	40.88	66.28	91.68	117.08	142.48	167.88
5/8	15.87	41.27	66.67	92.07	117.47	142.87	168.27
41/64	16.27	41.67	67.07	92.47	117.87	143.27	168.67
21/32	16.67	42.07	67.47	92.87	118.27	143.67	169.07
43/64	17.07	42.46	67.86	93.26	118.66	144.06	169.46
11/16	17.46	42.86	68.26	93.66	119.06	144.46	169.86
45/64	17.86	43.26	68.66	94.06	119.46	144.86	170.26
23/32	18.26	43.66	69.05	94.45	119.85	145.25	170.65
47/64	18.65	44.05	69.45	94.85	120.25	145.65	171.05
3/4	19.05	44.45	69.85	95.25	120.65	146.05	171.45
49/64	19.45	44.85	70.25	95.65	121.04	146.44	171.84
25/32	19.84	45.24	70.64	96.04	121.44	146.84	172.24
51/64	20.24	45.64	71.04	96.44	121.84	147.24	172.64
13/16	20.64	46.04	71.44	96.84	122.24	147.63	173.03
53/64	21.03	46.43	71.83	97.23	122.63	148.03	173.43
27/32	21.43	46.83	72.23	97.63	123.03	148.43	173.83
55/64	21.83	47.23	72.63	98.03	123.43	148.83	174.22
7/8	22.22	47.62	73.02	98.42	123.82	149.22	174.62
57/64	22.62	48.02	73.42	98.82	124.22	149.62	175.02
29/32	23.02	48.42	73.82	99.22	124.62	150.02	175.42
59/64	23.42	48.81	74.21	99.61	125.01	150.41	175.81
15/16	23.81	49.21	74.61	100.01	125.41	150.81	176.21
61/64	24.21	49.61	75.01	100.41	125.81	151.21	176.61
31/32	24.61	50.01	75.4	100.8	126.2	151.6	177.
63/64	25.	50.4	75.8	101.2	126.6	152.	177.4

Inches	0	1	2	3	4	5	6
		25.4	50.8	76.2	101.6	127.	152.4
1/64	0.40	25.80	51.20	76.60	102.	127.39	152.79
1/32	0.79	26.19	51.59	76.99	102.39	127.79	153.19
3/64	1.19	26.59	51.99	77.39	102.79	128.19	153.59
1/16	1.59	26.99	52.39	77.79	103.19	128.59	153.98
5/64	1.98	27.38	52.78	78.18	103.58	128.98	154.38
3/32	2.38	27.78	53.18	78.58	103.98	129.38	154.78
7/64	2.77	28.17	53.58	78.98	104.37	129.78	155.18
1/8	3.17	28.57	53.97	79.37	104.77	130.17	155.57
9/64	3.57	28.97	54.37	79.77	105.17	130.57	155.97
5/32	3.97	29.37	54.77	80.17	105.57	130.97	156.37
11/64	4.37	29.76	55.16	80.56	105.96	131.36	156.76
3/16	4.76	30.16	55.56	80.96	106.36	131.76	157.16
13/64	5.16	30.56	55.96	81.36	106.76	132.16	157.56
7/32	5.56	30.96	56.36	81.75	107.16	132.55	157.95
15/64	5.95	31.35	56.75	82.15	107.55	132.95	158.35
1/4	6.35	31.75	57.15	82.55	107.95	133.35	158.75
17/64	6.75	32.15	57.55	82.95	108.34	133.74	159.14
9/32	7.14	32.54	57.94	83.34	108.74	134.14	159.54
19/64	7.54	32.94	58.34	83.74	109.14	134.54	159.94
5/16	7.94	33.34	58.74	84.14	109.54	134.94	160.33
21/64	8.33	33.73	59.13	84.53	109.93	135.33	160.73
11/32	8.73	34.13	59.53	84.93	110.33	135.73	161.13
23/64	9.13	34.53	59.93	85.33	110.73	136.13	161.53
3/8	9.52	34.92	60.32	85.72	111.12	136.52	161.92
25/64	9.92	35.32	60.72	86.12	111.52	136.92	162.32
13/32	10.32	35.72	61.12	86.52	111.92	137.32	162.72
27/64	10.72	36.11	61.51	86.91	112.31	137.71	163.11
7/16	11.11	36.51	61.91	87.31	112.71	138.11	163.51
29/64	11.51	36.91	62.31	87.71	113.11	138.51	163.91
15/32	11.91	37.31	62.71	88.1	113.5	138.9	164.3
31/64	12.3	37.7	63.1	88.5	113.9	139.3	164.7

Appendix C

DECIMAL EQUIVALENTS OF MILLIMETRES

Millimetres Expressed in Inches

MM	0.1	1	10	20	30	40
			.3937	.7874	1.1811	1.5748
1	.0039	.0394	.4331	.8268	1.2205	1.6142
2	.0079	.0787	.4724	.8661	1.2598	1.6535
3	.0118	.1181	.5118	.9055	1.2992	1.6929
4	.0157	.1575	.5512	.9449	1.3386	1.7323
5	.0197	.1968	.5905	.9842	1.3779	1.7716
6	.0236	.2362	.6299	1.0236	1.4173	1.8110
7	.0276	.2756	.6693	1.0630	1.4567	1.8504
8	.0315	.3150	.7087	1.1024	1.4961	1.8898
9	.0354	.3543	.7480	1.1417	1.5354	1.9291

MM	50	60	70	80	90	100
	1.9685	2.3622	2.7559	3.1496	3.5433	3.9370
1	2.0079	2.4016	2.7953	3.1890	3.5827	3.9764
2	2.0472	2.4409	2.8346	3.2283	3.6220	4.0157
3	2.0866	2.4803	2.8740	3.2677	3.6614	4.0551
4	2.1260	2.5197	2.9134	3.3071	3.7008	4.0945
5	2.1653	2.5590	2.9527	3.3464	3.7401	4.1338
6	2.2047	2.5984	2.9921	3.3858	3.7795	4.1732
7	2.2441	2.6378	3.0315	3.4252	3.8189	4.2126
8	2.2835	2.6772	3.0709	3.4646	3.8583	4.2520
9	2.3228	2.7165	3.1102	3.5039	3.8976	4.2913

Appendix D

TEMPERATURE CONVERSION TABLE

Degrees Celsius (°C); Degrees Fahrenheit (°F)

Deg. C.	Deg. F.	Deg. C.	Deg. F.	Deg. C.	Deg. F.	Deg. C.	Deg. F.	Deg. C.	Deg. F.
− 40	− 40.0	8	46.4	56	132.8	104	219.2	152	305.6
− 39	− 38.2	9	48.2	57	134.6	105	221.0	153	307.4
− 38	− 36.4	10	50.0	58	136.4	106	222.8	154	309.2
− 37	− 34.6	11	51.8	59	138.2	107	224.6	155	311.0
− 36	− 32.8	12	53.6	60	140.0	108	226.4	156	312.8
− 35	− 31.0	13	55.4	61	141.8	109	228.2	157	314.6
− 34	− 29.2	14	57.2	62	143.6	110	230.0	158	316.4
− 33	− 27.4	15	59.0	63	145.4	111	231.8	159	318.2
− 32	− 25.6	16	60.8	64	147.2	112	233.6	160	320.0
− 31	− 23.8	17	52.6	65	149.0	113	235.4	161	321.8
− 30	− 22.0	18	64.4	66	150.8	114	237.2	162	323.6
− 29	− 20.2	19	66.2	67	152.6	115	239.0	163	325.4
− 28	− 18.4	20	68.0	68	154.4	116	240.8	164	327.2
− 27	− 16.6	21	69.8	69	156.2	117	242.6	165	329.0
− 26	− 14.8	22	71.6	70	158.0	118	244.4	166	330.8
− 25	− 13.0	23	73.4	71	159.8	119	246.2	167	332.6
− 24	− 11.2	24	75.2	72	161.6	120	248.0	168	334.4
− 23	− 9.4	25	77.0	73	163.4	121	249.8	169	336.2
− 22	− 7.6	26	78.8	74	165.2	122	251.6	170	338.0
− 21	− 5.8	27	80.6	75	167.0	123	253.4	171	339.8
− 20	− 4.0	28	82.4	76	168.8	124	255.2	172	341.6
− 19	− 2.2	29	84.2	77	170.6	125	257.0	173	343.4
− 18	− 0.4	30	86.0	78	172.4	126	258.8	174	345.2
− 17	+ 1.4	31	87.8	79	174.2	127	260.6	175	347.0
− 16	3.2	32	89.6	80	176.0	128	262.4	176	348.8
− 15	5.0	33	91.4	81	177.8	129	264.2	177	350.6
− 14	6.8	34	93.2	82	179.6	130	266.0	178	352.4
− 13	8.6	35	95.0	83	181.4	131	267.8	179	354.2
− 12	10.4	36	96.8	84	183.2	132	269.6	180	356.0
− 11	12.2	37	98.6	85	185.0	133	271.4	181	357.8
− 10	14.0	38	100.4	86	186.8	134	273.2	182	359.6
− 9	15.8	39	102.2	87	188.6	135	275.0	183	361.4
− 8	17.6	40	104.0	88	190.4	136	276.8	184	363.2
− 7	19.4	41	105.8	89	192.2	137	278.6	185	365.0
− 6	21.2	42	107.6	90	194.0	138	280.4	186	366.8
− 5	23.0	43	109.4	91	195.8	139	282.2	187	368.6
− 4	24.8	44	111.2	92	197.6	140	284.0	188	370.4
− 3	26.6	45	113.0	93	199.4	141	285.8	189	372.2
− 2	28.4	46	114.8	94	201.2	142	287.6	190	374.0
− 1	30.2	47	116.6	95	203.0	143	285.4	191	375.8
0	32.0	48	118.4	96	204.8	144	291.2	192	377.6
+ 1	33.8	49	120.2	97	206.6	145	293.0	193	379.4
2	35.6	50	122.0	98	208.4	146	294.8	194	381.2
3	37.4	51	123.8	99	210.2	147	296.6	195	383.0
4	39.2	52	125.6	100	212.0	148	298.4	196	384.8
5	41.0	53	127.4	101	213.8	149	300.2	197	386.6
6	42.8	54	129.2	102	215.6	150	302.0	198	388.4
7	44.6	55	131.0	103	217.4	151	303.8	199	390.2

Appendix E

GEOMETRIC FORMULAS

Circle:

Area of circle $= \pi r^2$

Circumference of
circle $= 2\pi r = \pi d$

Sphere:

Surface area of
sphere $= 4\pi r^2 = \pi d^2$

Volume of sphere $= \frac{4}{3}\pi r^3 = 0.5236 d^3$

Cube:

Area of cube $= 6a^2$

Volume of cube $= a^3$

Cylinder:

Lateral surface area
of cylinder $= 2\pi rh = \pi dh$

Area of base $= \pi r^2$

Area of closed
cylinder (total
surface area) $= 2\pi r\,(h+r) = \pi d\,(h+r)$

Volume of cylinder $= \pi r^2 h$

Cone:

Lateral area of
cone $= \pi r \times$ slant height

Area of base $= \pi r^2$

Volume of cone $= \frac{1}{3}\pi r^2 h$

Note:

r $=$ radius
d $=$ diameter
π $= 3.1416$
a $=$ length of one side of cube
h $=$ height

Appendix F

CIRCUMFERENCES AND AREAS OF CIRCLES

Diam. in inches	Circum. in inches	Area in sq. in.
1/64	.04909	.00019
1/32	.09818	.00077
3/64	.14726	.00173
1/16	.19635	.00307
3/32	29452	.00690
1/8	.39270	.01227
3/32	.49087	.01917
1/16	.58905	.02761
3/32	.68722	.03758
1/4	.78540	.04909
9/32	.88357	.06213
5/16	.98175	.07670
11/32	1.0799	.09281
3/8	1.1781	.11045
13/32	1.2763	.12962
7/16	1.3744	.15033
15/32	1.4726	.17257
1/2	1.5708	.19635
17/32	1.6690	.22166
9/16	1.7671	.24850
19/32	1.8653	.27688
5/8	1.9635	.30680
21/32	2.0617	.33824
11/16	2.1598	.37122
23/32	2.2580	.40574
3/4	2.3562	.44179
25/32	2.4544	.47937
13/16	2.5525	.51849
27/32	2.6507	.55914
7/8	2.7489	.60132
29/32	2.8471	.64504
15/16	2.9452	.69029
31/32	3.0434	.73708
1	3.1416	7854
1/16	3.3379	.8866
1/8	3.5343	.9940
3/16	3.7306	1.1075
1/4	3.9270	1.2272
5/16	4.1233	1.3530
3/8	4.3197	1.4849
7/16	4.5160	1.6230
1/2	4.7124	1.7671
9/16	4.9087	1.9175
5/8	5.1051	2.0739
11/16	5.3014	2.2365
3/4	5.4978	2.4053
13/16	5.6941	2.5802
7/8	5.8905	2.7612
15/16	6.0868	2.9483
2	6.2832	3.1416
1/16	6.4795	3.3410
1/8	6.6759	3.5466
3/16	6.8722	3.7583
1/4	7.0686	3.9761
5/16	7.2649	4.2000
3/8	7.4613	4.4301
7/16	7.6576	4.6664
2 1/2	7.8540	4.9087
9/16	8.0503	5.1572
5/8	8.2467	5.4119
11/16	8.4430	5.6727
3/4	8.6394	5.9396
13/16	8.8357	6.2126
7/8	9.0321	6.4918
15/16	9.2284	6.7771
3	9.4248	7.0686
1/16	9.6211	7.3662
1/8	9.8175	7.6699
3/16	10.014	7.9798
1/4	10.210	8.2958
5/16	10.407	8.6179
3/8	10.603	8.9462
7/16	10.799	9.2806
1/2	10.996	9.6211
9/16	11.192	9.9678
5/8	11.388	10.321
11/16	11.585	10.680
3/4	11.781	11.045
13/16	11.977	11.416
7/8	12.174	11.793
15/16	12.370	12.177
4	12.566	12.566
1/16	12.763	12.962
1/8	12.959	13.364
3/16	13.155	13.772
1/4	13.352	14.186
5/16	13.548	14.607
3/8	13.744	15.033
7/16	13.941	15.466
1/2	14.137	15.904
9/16	14.334	16.349
5/8	14.530	16.800
11/16	14.726	17.257
3/4	14.923	17.728
13/16	15.119	18.190
7/8	15.315	18.665
15/16	15.512	19.147
5	15.708	19.635
1/16	15.904	20.129
1/8	16.101	20.629
3/16	16.297	21.135
1/4	16.493	21.648
5/16	16.690	22.166
3/8	16.886	22.691
7/16	17.082	23.221
1/2	17.279	23.758
9/16	17.475	24.301
5/8	17.671	24.850
11/16	17.868	25.406
3/4	18.064	25.967
13/16	18.261	26.535
7/8	18.457	27.109
15/16	18.653	27.688
6	18.850	28.274
1/8	19.242	29.465
6 1/4	19.635	30.680
3/8	20.028	31.919
1/2	20.420	33.183
5/8	20.813	34.472
3/4	21.206	35.785
7/8	21.598	37.122
7	21.991	38.485
1/8	22.384	39.871
1/4	22.776	41.282
3/8	23.169	42.718
1/2	23.562	44.179
5/8	23.955	45.664
3/4	24.347	47.173
7/8	24.740	48.707
8	25.133	50.265
1/8	25.525	51.849
1/4	25.918	53.456
3/8	26.311	55.088
1/2	26.704	56.745
5/8	27.096	58.426
3/4	27.489	60.132
7/8	27.882	61.862
9	28.274	63.617
1/8	28.667	65.397
1/4	29.060	67.201
3/8	29.452	69.029
1/2	29.845	70.882
5/8	30.238	72.760
3/4	30.631	74.662
7/8	31.023	76.589
10	31.416	78.540
1/8	31.809	80.516
1/4	32.201	82.516
3/8	32.594	84.541
1/2	32.987	86.590
5/8	33.379	88.664
3/4	33.772	90.763
7/8	34.165	92.886
11	34.558	95.033
1/8	34.950	97.205
1/4	35.343	99.402
3/8	35.736	101.62
1/2	36.128	103.87
5/8	36.521	106.14
3/4	36.914	108.43
7/8	37.306	110.75
12	37.699	113.10
1/8	38.092	115.47
1/4	38.485	117.86
3/8	38.877	120.28
1/2	39.270	122.72
5/8	39.663	125.19
3/4	40.055	127.68
7/8	40.448	130.19
13	40.841	132.73
1/8	41.233	135.30
1/4	41.626	137.89
3/8	42.019	140.50
1/2	42.412	143.14

Appendix G

METRIC AND DECIMAL EQUIVALENTS OF COMMON FRACTIONS

Fractions of an Inch	Decimals of an Inch	Milli-metres	Fractions of an Inch	Decimals of an Inch	Milli-metres
1/64	.0156	0.397	33/64	.5156	13.097
1/32	.0313	0.794	17/32	.5313	13.494
3/64	.0469	1.191	35/64	.5469	13.891
1/16	.0625	1.588	9/16	.5625	14.287
5/64	.0781	1.985	37/64	.5781	14.684
3/32	.0938	2.381	19/32	.5938	15.081
7/64	.1094	2.778	39/64	.6094	15.478
1/8	.1250	3.175	5/8	.6250	15.875
9/64	.1406	3.572	41/64	.6406	16.272
5/32	.1563	3.969	21/32	.6563	16.688
11/64	.1719	4.366	43/64	.6719	17.085
3/16	.1875	4.762	11/16	.6875	17.462
13/64	.2031	5.159	45/64	.7031	17.859
7/32	.2188	5.556	23/32	.7188	18.256
15/64	.2344	5.953	47/64	.7344	18.653
1/4	.2500	6.350	3/4	.7500	19.050
17/64	.2656	6.747	49/64	.7645	19.447
9/32	.2813	7.144	25/32	.7813	19.843
19/64	.2969	7.541	51/64	.7969	20.240
5/16	.3135	7.937	13/16	.8125	20.637
21/64	.3281	8.334	53/64	.8281	21.034
11/32	.3438	8.731	27/32	.8438	21.430
23/64	.3594	9.128	55/64	.8594	21.827
3/8	.3750	9.525	7/8	.8750	22.224
25/64	.3906	9.922	57/64	.8906	22.621
13/32	.4063	10.319	29/32	.9063	23.018
27/64	.4219	10.716	59/64	.9219	23.415
7/16	.4375	11.112	15/16	.9375	23.812
29/64	.4531	11.509	61/64	.9531	24.209
15/32	.4688	11.906	31/32	.9688	24.606
31/64	.4844	12.303	63/64	.9844	25.003
1/2	.5000	12.700	1	1.0000	25.400

Appendix H

DECIMAL EQUIVALENTS OF TWIST DRILLS

Size	Drill Diameter	Size	Drill Diameter	Size	Drill Diameter	Size	Drill Diameter	Size	Drill Diameter
				NUMBER DRILLS					
1	.2280	17	.1730	33	.1130	49	.0730	65	.0350
2	.2210	18	.1695	34	.1110	50	.0700	66	.0330
3	.2130	19	.1660	35	.1100	51	.0670	67	.0320
4	.2090	20	.1610	36	.1065	52	.0635	68	.0310
5	.2055	21	.1590	37	.1040	53	.0595	69	.0292
6	.2040	22	.1570	38	.1015	54	.0550	70	.0280
7	.2010	23	.1540	39	.0995	55	.0520	71	.0260
8	.1990	24	.1520	40	.0980	56	.0465	72	.0250
9	.1960	25	.1495	41	.0960	57	.0430	73	.0240
10	1935	26	.1470	42	.0935	58	.0420	74	.0225
11	.1910	27	.1440	43	.0890	59	.0410	75	.0210
12	1890	28	.1405	44	.0860	60	.0400	76	0200
13	.1850	29	.1360	45	.0820	61	.0390	77	.0180
14	.1820	30	.1285	46	.0810	62	.0380	78	.0160
15	.1800	31	.1200	47	.0785	63	.0370	79	.0145
16	.1770	32	.1160	48	.0760	64	.0360	80	.0135

Size	Drill Diameter	Size	Drill Diameter	Size	Drill Diameter	Size	Drill Diameter	Size	Drill Diameter
				LETTER DRILLS					
A	.234	G	.261	L	.290	Q	.332	V	.377
B	.238	H	.266	M	.295	R	.339	W	.386
C	.242	I	.272	N	.302	S	.348	X	.397
D	.246	J	.277	O	.316	T	.358	Y	404
E	.250	K	281	P	.323	U	.368	Z	413
F	.257								

Appendix I

TAP DRILL SIZES

American Standard Coarse-Thread Series				American Standard Fine-Thread Series			
Size	Threads per Inch	Tap Drill Size	Drill Diameter	Size	Threads per Inch	Tap Drill Size	Drill Diameter
1	64	No. 53	.0595	0	80	$\frac{3}{64}$	.0469
2	56	No. 50	.0700	1	72	No. 53	.0595
3	48	No. 47	.0785	2	64	No. 50	.0700
4	40	No. 43	.0890	3	56	No. 45	.0820
5	40	No. 38	.1015	4	48	No. 42	.0935
6	32	No. 36	.1065	5	44	No. 37	.1040
8	32	No. 29	.1360	6	40	No. 33	.1130
10	24	No. 25	.1495	8	36	No. 29	.1360
12	24	No. 16	.1770	10	32	No. 21	.1590
$\frac{1}{4}$	20	No. 7	.2010	12	28	No. 14	.1820
$\frac{5}{16}$	18	F	.2570	$\frac{1}{4}$	28	3	.2130
$\frac{3}{8}$	16	$\frac{5}{16}$	.3125	$\frac{5}{16}$	24	I	.2720
$\frac{7}{16}$	14	U	.3680	$\frac{3}{8}$	24	Q	.3320
$\frac{1}{2}$	13	$\frac{27}{64}$	.4219	$\frac{7}{16}$	20	$\frac{25}{64}$	.3906
$\frac{9}{16}$	12	$\frac{31}{64}$	.4844	$\frac{1}{2}$	20	$\frac{29}{64}$	.4531
$\frac{5}{8}$	11	$\frac{17}{32}$	.5312	$\frac{9}{16}$	18	$\frac{33}{64}$	.5156
$\frac{3}{4}$	10	$\frac{21}{32}$	.6562	$\frac{5}{8}$	18	$\frac{37}{64}$	.5781
$\frac{7}{8}$	9	$\frac{49}{64}$	.7656	$\frac{3}{4}$	16	$\frac{11}{16}$	.6875
1	8	$\frac{7}{8}$	.8750	$\frac{7}{8}$	14	$\frac{13}{16}$	.8125
				1	14	$\frac{15}{16}$	.9375

The tap drills listed are commercial sizes based upon an average of 75% thread depth.

Appendix J

STANDARD PIPE DIMENSIONS FOR TAP DRILLS

Pipe Size	Outside Diameter	Inside Diameter	Tap Drill	Tap Depth	Inside Area	Threads per Inch
$\frac{1}{8}$	.405	.269	#R (.339)	$\frac{1}{4}$	.057	27
$\frac{1}{4}$	.540	.364	$\frac{7}{16}$	$\frac{3}{8}$	.104	18
$\frac{3}{8}$	.675	.493	$\frac{37}{64}$	$\frac{3}{8}$	.191	18
$\frac{1}{2}$	.840	.622	$\frac{23}{32}$	$\frac{1}{2}$	.304	14
$\frac{3}{4}$	1.050	.824	$\frac{59}{64}$	$\frac{9}{16}$	.533	14
1	1.315	1.049	$1\frac{5}{32}$	$\frac{11}{16}$	.864	$11\frac{1}{2}$
$1\frac{1}{4}$	1.660	1.380	$1\frac{1}{2}$	$\frac{11}{16}$	1.495	$11\frac{1}{2}$
$1\frac{1}{2}$	1.900	1.610	$1\frac{47}{64}$	$\frac{11}{16}$	2.036	$11\frac{1}{2}$

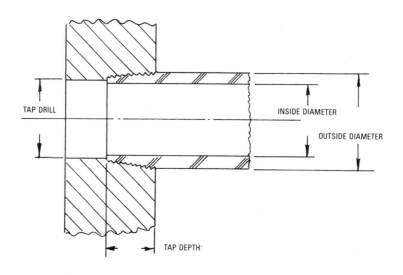

Appendix K

RECOMMENDED DRILL SPEEDS IN FEET PER MINUTE

Material	High-Speed–Steel Drills Minimum to Maximum	Carbide Drills Minimum to Maximum
Aluminum	150–300	230–450
Brass and bronze	150–300	230–450
Cast iron	60–90	100–150
Copper	70–100	120–170
Forged steel	40–70	70–130
General purpose steel	70–100	120–170
High-carbon steel	40–70	70–130
Plastics	100–200	150–300
Stainless steel	30–70	50–130
Wood	200–300	300–450

Appendix L

DRILL SIZES AND CUTTING SPEEDS

Drill Size in Inches	Feet per Minute							
	30	40	50	60	70	80	90	100
	Revolutions per Minute							
$\frac{1}{16}$	1800	2400	3000	3700	4300	5000	5500	6100
$\frac{1}{8}$	900	1200	1500	1850	2150	2500	2750	3050
$\frac{3}{16}$	600	800	1000	1200	1400	1600	1800	2000
$\frac{1}{4}$	450	600	700	900	1000	1200	1400	1500
$\frac{5}{16}$	360	500	600	700	850	1000	1100	1200
$\frac{3}{8}$	300	400	500	600	700	800	900	1000
$\frac{7}{16}$	260	350	440	530	610	700	790	870
$\frac{1}{2}$	230	300	380	460	540	610	690	760
$\frac{5}{8}$	180	240	300	360	430	490	550	610
$\frac{3}{4}$	150	200	250	300	350	400	450	500
$\frac{7}{8}$	130	180	220	260	300	350	400	440
1	110	150	190	230	270	300	340	380

Index

Other Books of Interest

- *Making Wood Signs*
  Woods for Sign-Making
  Designing Wood Signs
  Basic Tools and Machines
  Cutout Letters
  Hand-Carved Signs
  Routed Signs
  Sign Routing and Carving Machines
  Making Large Signs
  Making a Huge Sign
  Sandblasting Signs
  Finishing Signs
  Alphabets
  Keeping Tools Sharp

- *Router Handbook*
  Router Basics
  Router Bits
  Safety and Maintenance
  Basic Routing Operations
  Pattern and Template Routing
  Routing Joints and Surfaces
  Freehand Routing
  Routing Plastic Laminates
  Sign-Making Router Accessories
  A Variety of Router Accessories
  Router Dovetailing
  Overarm and Pin-Routing Machines
  Router Carving Machines
  User-Made Jigs and Fixtures
  Panel Routing Devices
  Project Section